Le Road Trip

When Wanderers
Cease to Roam
A Traveler's Journal of Staying Put

❦ Le Road Trip ❦

A Traveler's Journal of Love and France

Vivian Swift

BLOOMSBURY

New York   Berlin   London   Sydney

Published by Bloomsbury USA, New York

All papers used by Bloomsbury USA are natural, recyclable products made from wood grown in well-managed forests. The manufacturing processes conform to the environmental regulations of the country of origin.

LIBRARY OF CONGRESS CATALOGING-IN-PUBLICATION DATA HAS BEEN APPLIED FOR.

ISBN: 978-1-60819-532-9

First U.S. Edition 2012

3 5 7 9 10 8 6 4 2

The entire text of this book has been typeset by hand by the author.
Printed and bound in China by C&C Offset Printing Co Ltd

How to Use This Book

- Hold upright, turn one page at a time.
- Keep dry: although this book makes a great dining companion, avoid dripping condiments or sauces onto the binding.
- Do not use as tinder, a flotation devise, or bait.
- Each chapter contains general travel advice, tips, and instructions as well as guidance specifically related to enjoying a meander around France; please read this book *before* or *after* your own journey -- not **during**.
  1. This is not a book with a lot of really useful information in it.
  2. No hotel or restaurant addresses are listed here; what -- do I look like Rick Steves?
  3. It's more of an "Art of Travel" kind of book.
  4. Hence all these pretty illustrations to inspire you to plan for your own adventure, or to help you remember your own fabulous experiences.
- When you get to the last page, close cover and return to upright position. If you simply *must* have an electronic component to this reading experience, you can look me up at my website:

  www.vivianswift.net.

DEDICATED
to
James Stone

Road Philosopher

Thank you for enlightening me on
the difference between:
Jean-Paul Sartre and Jerry Garcia (none),
good wine and swill
(if it doesn't come from Bordeaux it's not worth drinking),
. and
a good road trip and a great one,
(YOU).

Every road trip has its ups and downs,
just like a love affair, or the stock market.

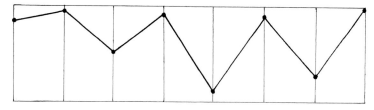

But more like a love affair.

Contents

TRAVEL.

Yes, we all do it. But some of us do it better than others. This is where I come in.

I wouldn't call myself a **travel expert**, but that's just me being modest. OF COURSE I'm a travel expert.

I've been traveling for 30 years and been to 40 countries without ONCE going on a cruise. Yes, I'm bragging. I've stayed in over 50 youth hostels without *ever* getting thrown up on. I've eaten local delicacies, from brains to fried grasshoppers to goat (with my bare hands) to Amazonian BBQ (God knows what was on *that* grill. *"Is that an ear?"* I asked the cook. "Yeah, sure," he said, so shiftily that I began to worry that **ear** could be a euphemism for something even more unthinkable. That's when I learned that there can never be a good answer to the question, *Is that an ear?).* I've been bitten by malarial mosquitoes, threatened by wild baboons, stalked by loose moose, and proposed to by a drunken African soldier who broke into my bedroom in the middle of the night. I've traipsed in elephant dung and human turds and squished myself into rattle-trap *taxis-brousses* with snotty babies and leprous beggars. I've dodged the leering bachelors of Rome, side-stepped camel spit in Ouagadougou, and stared down the judgmental gaze of Parisians. And through it all I've never been hospitalized, jailed, stranded, pierced, tattooed, or ransomed. That's how good I am.

My motto is:
Whatever Doesn't Make You Go Home Makes You Stronger.

It was during my most recent return trip to France -- you could call it a honeymoon; that's what my new husband called it -- that I congratulated myself on how well I was managing things. Much flattered by my own praise, I told myself, "**You should write a book!**"

And that's what I did.

Although this book takes place in France, it's not *about* France, except for the hundreds of illustrations and equal number of notes and captions and stories.

OK, it's a little bit about France.

Actually, kind of a *lot* about France.

But mostly it's about **travel**.

Everybody does it these days, so much so that one out of every ten jobs in the global economy is travel-related. On any given day in America there are 1.8 million people lining up for 30,000 flights in 450 domestic airports. This book is about travel as its own activity, with its own customs and its own history that has been passed down from generation to generation, about travel as a pastime as different from ordinary life as baseball is to ballroom dancing. It's about travel as *that thing* we do in between buying souvenirs and posing for photos in front of tourist attractions; it's *that thing* we fantasize about when we are sick of our jobs, fed up with our families, and bored with ourselves.

Travel is a lot like sex: it's very personal, prone to fads, and competitive; and we're all secretly curious about how other people do it.

Here's how *I* do it.

Phase One: Anticipation

In love and travel
getting there is half the fun.

Anticipation. In love and travel, getting there is half the fun.
The lustful impatience, the passionate daydreams,
the nerve-wracking *waiting*...lovers and travelers
are all alike when they find themselves on the brink of a new adventure.

Love
Scientists and romantics say ANTICIPATION is a crucial phase of the mating process. We need to get revved up, hit with a dose of spine-tingling, hand-sweating, heart-pounding **desire** to force us to overcome our natural instincts to just stay home and watch TV in our jammies. It's what makes us **get up and get out** there.

Travel
ANTICIPATION is a crucial phase of any journey. It's the promise that life will be different, *better*, for having seen an amazing sunset over the pyramids of Egypt, for dining on gourmet delicacies in Burgundy, for experiencing the stillness in a Zen temple in Kyoto. We want the same thing from **travel** that we want from love: a life-changing encounter with destiny. Plus fantastic scenery.

When I was 19 years old
I worked in the office of a factory that made industrial gauges. All day long I filled out shipping forms, by hand, in pencil, which I then handed over to a *skilled* worker --the typist.

I understood, from the names on these shipping forms, that gauges were used to manu-facture a variety of liquid and gassy things, from beer to chemical weapons.

Gauges. They are a dreary way to view the wonders and evils of human enterprise.

It was my first day back at work after the New Year holidays of 1975. I stared at a stack of shipping forms and suddenly knew that I had to quit this life. I had to go to **Paris**.

I ripped the shrink wrap off the new page-a-day calendar on my desk, took my pencil, and began to hand-number the pages. I penciled in every number from 1 to 209. There it was: I had 209 days to go until the two-week Summer hiatus when the factory shut down, stopped making gauges, and every employee was sent on a 14-day vacation.

That day, July 28, 1975, the 209th day of the year, was going to be the day that I took off for **Paris**. That day was going to be the first day of the rest of my life.

So day by day, as I wore down my pencils and filled up reams of shipping forms, I would check the countdown on my calendar, and imagine myself 209 days from now, 152 days from now, 64 days from now...

Talk about **anticipation**. For 209 days, that's all I *lived* on.

Sail away from the safe harbor.
Catch the Trade winds in your sails.
Explore. Dream. Discover.

Mark Twain (1835 - 1910)

Congratulations!
You've answered the call for adventure!
Now, here's how to prepare for it:

What to Pack

Citizen of the World Jacket
A traveler needs pockets. And something that looks good even after you've had to sleep in it in a fleabag hotel in Bordeaux.

Culturally Sensitive Sweater
A cashmere pullover (several sizes too big) looks *très chic* when worn over the shoulders of a cute Summer frock on a cool Paris night and *très* sensible when layered for warmth under your travel-worn jacket for a hike in the Breton woods.

Yes. All this stuff will fit ← into this carry-on bag.

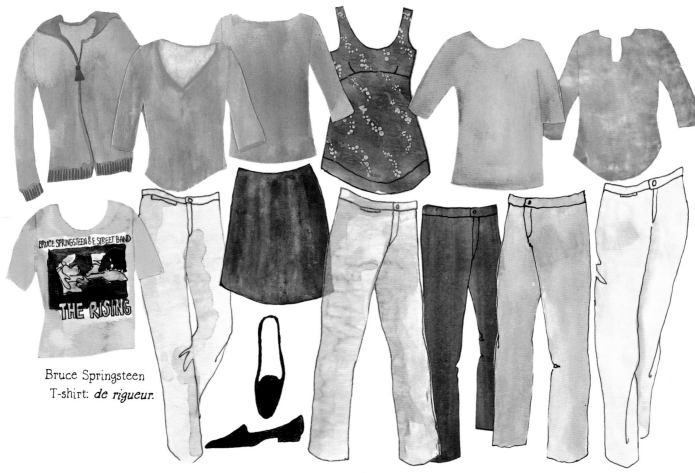

Bruce Springsteen T-shirt: *de rigueur.*

The Vivian Swift Philosophy of Packing:

Pack for the person you are on Saturday morning.
Whatever you wear when dashing out on your Saturday morning errands --

- **heading out** to the bookstore to pick up that volume of Song Dynasty poetry that you special ordered, or
- **stopping in** at the Piggly Wiggly to get the ingredients for your barbeque sauce (secret recipe), or
- **staggering** to the corner deli for a pack of breakfast cigarettes, or
- **dropping by** the tack department at Hermes to look for a new saddle for your polo pony . . .

. . .whatever your Saturday morning style is,
that's what you should be wearing on the road.

Your Saturday morning clothes are the garments that you put on automatically, the duds that you wear without thinking. That's the kind of comfort you need when traveling.

What you wear on Saturday morning shows the world your personal style, tells the truth about what best represents your most authentic self.

That's who you need to be on the road.

How to Live Out of a Suitcase

How well you travel -- that is, how quickly you can change course, how far you go on spur-of-the-moment decisions, how happily you wander from here to there -- depends on how easily you can carry your biggest burden: **your luggage.**

- A carry-on suitcase easily holds a 28-day wardrobe.
- On the road, plan to wear every article of outer clothing a minimum of four times.
- 28 days divided by a four-day cycle equals seven changes of outfits.
- After a trip to a laundromat (a delightful cultural experience in any foreign country) you're ready for another 28 days.
- And the next 28 days, and the next. Indefinitely.
- The point of "traveling light" isn't to cram as much stuff as possible into a small bag.
- Rather, it's discovering how little you really need in order to have the time of your life.

Consider the Cape
John Ledyard (1751 - 1789) called himself "the greatest traveler in history." In his brief life he traversed more of the Earth's surface than any other man of his time.

He was also, quite certainly, one of the greatest **packers** in history.

After sailing around the world as a crewman on the *Resolution* for Captain Cook for four years (from 1776 to 1780) Ledyard's next adventure was to made good on his lifelong dream of walking around the world. He started out from London in January 1786. He was 34 years old.

Ledyard walked for two years and 3,795 miles (6,106 km) before he was arrested in Yakutsk, by Catherine the Great, for being a spy. His entire wardrobe during this time (not counting his Siberian-made boots and trousers) consisted of little more than one change of socks, a shirt, and a cloak.

But what a cloak!
"I travelled on foot with it in Denmark, Sweden, Lapland, Finland, and the lord knows where." Ledyard praised his cloak in a letter to his brother in Connecticut: "I have slept in it, eat[en] in it, drank in it, fought in it, negotiated in it. Through every scene it has been my constant and hardy servant."

May your baggage be blessed with such worthy garb.

Everything that can add to your comfort I should recommend you to take. I had a portmanteau capable of containing 12 shirts and other things in proportion; a pair of canteens, containing breakfast and dinner conveniences for two; a saddle and a bridle;... *by all means carry tea*...a blanket is quite unnecessary; [take] two pairs of linen sheets, sewed up at each side and at one extremity, as a defense against vermin.
T. R. Joliffe
Letters From Egypt (1854)

Rice, Dahl, Ovaltine,
Spoons -- 3,
Smelling salts,
Nails of all sizes,
Safety pins,
A list of departed souls
V. R. Ragam, *Pilgrim's Travel Guide* (1963)

A Lady's List
A small flask of brandy
Smelling salts
Light literature
Cushions covered in chintz or satin
      for putting under the feet
Suede gloves in Summer
Woolen muffatees in Winter
Fine yellowish brown paper to line the
      drawers of inns: There is something
      not particularly tempting in the
      idea of placing one's possessions in
      a place where one does not know
      what preceded them.
Lillias Campbell Davidson
Hints to Lady Travellers at Home and Abroad (1889)

My Essentials

My Band-Aid
    box boudoir

Road Reading

The ashes of my cat,
    Winston

A Traveler's Scrapbook

Use adhesive tape to fasten
50 blank index cards together.
Trim ends of tape.

Make appropriate
accordion folds.

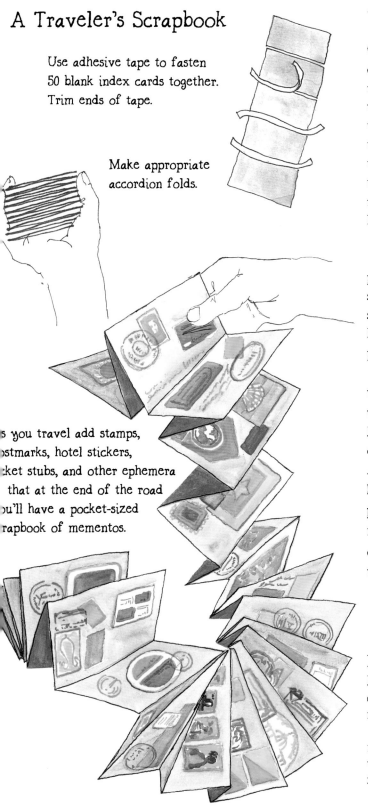

s you travel add stamps,
ostmarks, hotel stickers,
cket stubs, and other ephemera
 that at the end of the road
ou'll have a pocket-sized
rapbook of mementos.

Why Do We Travel?

Good question. Because the truth is that most of us should stay home -- so few people are really competent to travel. We all know it -- we've seen the lady in the skimpy minidress tottering across the Mer de Glace in high heels; the red-faced guy at the Pyramids fuming that there are no ice cubes in all of Egypt; the teenager sulking at the Great Wall because he'd rather be back home in Ohio, skateboarding with his friends, than *anywhere else in the freaking world with his parents.*

Why do we do it? For amusement, prestige, profit, education? Or because that's simply **what we do:** we **move**, sometimes onward, sometimes inward, always over the next hill or hurdle. Sometimes alone, sometimes with other people.

"Be remarkably cautious with regard to the choice of companion for a long journey," warned the old road tripper Count Leopold Berchtold (who amassed a wealth of travel advice during his 17-year-long journey from his home in Austria through the Turkish Empire, the Middle East, and North Africa): "If the person proposed is not exactly the same turn of mind he will be an intolerable burden -- a real obstruction to useful travels -- and convert the sweets of company into bitterness."

Count Leopold Berchtold,
*Essay to Direct and Extend the
Inquiries of Patriotic Travellers* (1789)

I prefer to travel solo. I agree with Count Leopold: a journey with the wrong traveling companion is torture every step of the way -- and most people are lousy traveling companions.

But then, a bit late in life, I met a man who made me think that he could be the kind of guy who would be good for the long haul. And good for a long road trip.

Unlikely Traveling Companions

Our paths did not cross that Summer of 1975.

Me: An anxious 19-year-old, making my way around Paris on a $10-a-day budget from money I'd saved from my factory job in Pennsylvania. My high school French (three years, B average) gets me in and out of museums and metro stations just fine. But do I dare to dream of more? I'm the first person in my family to get a passport, and it's just now dawning on me that I could go anywhere in the world from here. For now, though, I am content to sit quietly in the corner of a cheap student cafeteria with my *omelette nature*. Someday, however, I'll have the courage to face a professional Parisian waiter and *cervelle de veau au beurre noir.*

James: At age 22, already such a *bon vivant* that hitchhiking from Munich to Genoa with 20 cents in his pocket makes him feel *"carefree".* Four years of Episcopalian prep school French, C+ average, now just out of college (philosophy major) and passing through Paris on his way to his family's vacation home in Portugal. This rogue from Long Island is used to things "falling into place" (like the Summer before his sophomore year at Tulane, when he showed up at a Grateful Dead concert in San Francisco without tickets and got *miracled*). He's never spent a day feeling anxious, he tells me now, over whether his travels, or his life, would turn out OK.

30 Years Later

You never know who you'll end up marrying.

It was a rainy Thursday night in Manhattan during a cold Spring and, at a fine-arts fundraiser / cocktail party, I was looking at a room full of people I didn't know. A distinguished-looking silver-haired gentleman in a tweed jacket asked me if I was alone. "Yes," I said.

"So am I," he told me.

Small talk: he told me about the funeral that he'd been to that afternoon, I told him that I'd stopped off at a record shop on my way to the party to buy a Blow Monkeys CD.

Death and pop music from the 1980s are two of my favorite topics of conversation.

He liked that I had long hair and knew how to grade fancy colored diamonds. I liked his smile and, when he drank the caterer's weird-looking chocolate martinis, I liked his willingness to try new things.

We were married a year later.

And then we went to France.

September 2005

Le Road Trip

Paris • Normandy • Brittany • Bordeaux • Loire Valley • Chartres • Paris

Normandy	Brittany	Bordeaux	Loire Valley
Giverny	Pontorson	Bordeaux	Tours
Rouen	Mont-St-Michel	Saint-Emilion	Azay-le-Rideau
Bayeux	Saint-Malo	St-Philippe-d'Aiguilhe	Ussé
Omaha Beach	Cancale	La Réole	Langeais
	Fougères	Rauzan	Villandry
		Bergerac	Rivarennes
		Ste-Foy-la-Grand	Chinon
		St-Macaire	
		Margaux	
		St-Julien	
		Pauillac	
		Montalivet-les-Bains	
		Soulac-sur-Mer	
		Vertheuil	

Normandy

Brittany

Paris

Loire Valley

Bordeaux

Paris

Phase Two: Infatuation

Arrival: It's a lot like love at first sight.

Infatuation

To a traveler, every **arrival** is as if on a distant planet -- *that's why we travel.* To arrive as a new being in a new world, a world that will let us start over, as a better self, the person we've always wanted to be. That special joy that lights up our heart as we gaze at that new world with wild surmise?

It's a lot like love at first sight.

Love: Infatuation is the lunatic phase. *At long last!* you think to yourself: *I'm in love! I'm really in love!!* Your overwhelming delight in a new love makes you giddy, gullible, and stupid. Anybody who has ever fallen head over heels in love knows this is true. And it's **wonderful.** But maybe a little *too* wonderful.

Travel: That's also the way a traveler feels on the first day of a journey, the first day in a new country, a new city: Giddy, gullible, and stupid. So you might want to take some precautions against doing something *too* stupid in the first flush of travel-giddy foolishness. Such as:

Don't go shopping right away. In my 20s I was always rushing out to buy clothes in France, often spending money I couldn't afford, in my dash to **look** as French as I **felt.** I once paid $200 for a dress that I wore only twice. I finally took it to Africa with me when I joined the Peace Corps and it ended its days there, as the dress I wore when I scrubbed the floors in my hovel.

Don't dive into the local delicacies. I have nightmares when I think of all the street food I've scarfed down in foreign countries: fried grasshoppers, grilled fruit bat, roasted whole goat (that one I did with my bare hands), hasty snacks of boiled and deep-fried untranslatable things. These days I lose sleep thinking of yet-undiscovered deadly tropical diseases with decades-long incubation periods festering in my digestive tract, whose symptoms won't show up until I'm terminal. Hold off on the daredevil cuisine until you've sussed out all the pros and cons.

Don't get married. Sure, falling in love with foreigners is one of the happier hazards of travel. Just don't be in such an all-fire hurry to take it all the way to the altar.

On his first trip outside his native France, 26-year-old **Antoine de Saint-Exupéry** was the lone passenger on a small plane carrying mail from Paris to the Ivory Coast. Saint-Exupéry, who was to become one of the 20th century's greatest adventurers, had a most inauspicious initiation as a traveler, because near the end of this maiden voyage the pilot of the aircraft lost control of the plane. It plunged out of the sky and tumbled into the Sahara, crash-landing many miles short of its destination.

Saint-Exupéry, however, was so thrilled to have, at long last, ARRIVED in Africa!, that even sitting beside his wrecked plane, watching the sun set over the dunes as he waited for rescue, all he felt was **immense pride.** He writes:

"For the first time since I **was born it seemed to me that my life was my own and that I was responsible for it.**"

This happiness, this pride, struck the newly-arrived Saint-Exupéry (as he wrote in his memoir of his travels):

"like love itself."

Later in his life, Antoine de Saint-Exupéry (1900- 1944) would write the classic tale *The Little Prince,* a fable that begins with a similar **crash-landing** in the desert.

Paris

A Tale of Two Arrivals

Then, 1975

The French franc is worth 24 cents. The baguette I buy every other day for my lunch costs one franc. An omelet is 3.20 Fr and there are places where a glass of wine costs 90 centimes. For the first time in my life I don't mind being poor: it's so *picturesque* here.

With trembling anticipation I dip a *madeleine* into a cup of tea. I think hard, waiting for enlightenment. This can't be right. I take another bite of my tea-soaked cake. I write in my journal: "Tastes like string beans."

I begin to question my assumptions about European refinement when I see this sign at the entrance to Napoléon's Tomb:

> Ne crachez pas votre chewing-gum sur les moquettes. Merci!
>
> Bitte Spucken sie nicht ihren Kougummi auf den Tappich!
>
> Please, do not spit your chewing gum out on the carpets!

I see an elderly man on the street, his leg in a cast, and I think *"Must be a war wound."* When I think **war wound**, I'm thinking of WW II. Which ended 30 years ago. To say that I have **no sense of history** is an understatement.

Now, 2005

As the plane touches down at Charles de Gaulle airport, we dry our tears. The in-flight movie was a love story that made us both cry. I cried because I was so happy to be in my very own love story, with my new husband, on my way to Paris. My husband, James, cried because the movie was also about baseball and James loves baseball.

My first conversation on French soil goes like this: "There's no smoking allowed in the airport terminal," I say, in perfectly good French, to the woman who has lit up a Marlboro in the baggage claim area.

The woman looks at me sharply. I point to the sign: *Défense de Fumer.*

She answers me in mocking English. *"Zeez deestairb you?"* she says, exaggerating her astonishment that anyone would object to a little cigarette smoke for god's sake. With great disdain she drops the butt to the floor and crushes it with the patent leather toe of her tiny Roger Vivier ballerina flat.

I could *kiss* her -- for now I know that I have really and truly **arrived** in Paris!

On a scale of 1 to 5, adventure travelers rate France a 1 -- equal to Hawaii, New Zealand, and England (5 is reserved for the Arctic, Nepal, and Patagonia). But I wonder how many adventure travelers speak French? And how many of them insist, as James and I do, on talking to Parisians in their own language? Well, *you* try talking to Parisians when you know full well that they *hate* you for speaking their language with a foreign accent and are pretending not to understand a word you say -- and see if *you* wouldn't rather be in the Arctic, Nepal, or Patagonia.

From When We Were Young and Snobby.

Spartan Travel. For people like James and me, who started traveling in the 1970s when we were young and poor, luxury travel is a crime against authenticity. And worse: it's a waste of time. For us, frugality on the road enhances the quality of the experience of a foreign place.
Or, we could be full of beans and are just too *jejune* to check into a five-star hotel in Paris. I'll let you be the judge.

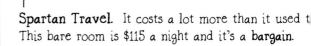

Spartan Travel. It costs a lot more than it used t
This bare room is $115 a night and it's a **bargain**.

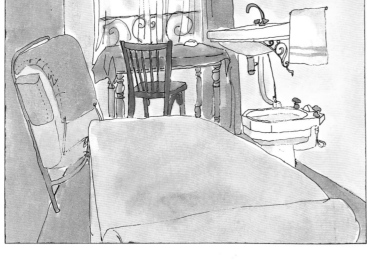

In 1975 my hotel room on the Rue du Lille cost $7.00 a night and included breakfast served on a tray in the hotel lobby. For *le petit déjeuner* I was given the choice of *café, thé,* or *chocolat,* the first time in my life that I'd ever been asked to even **conside** drinking **hot chocolate** at that time of day. Naturally, I came to think of hot chocolate as a very sophisticated morning drink and the fact that we'd never had hot chocolate at home for breakfas was just one more (France-inspired) discovery of m defective suburban American upbringing.

Along with the *bidet* and the sink in my room, ther was a skimpy hand towel and a tiny bar of Palmolive soap. There's a small bar of Palmolive soap in our 2005 hotel room too: that Palmolive smell, of pine-scented disinfectant overlaid with a heavy jasmine perfume, will forever remind me of Paris on $10.00 a day.

James and I are well aware of the toll that travelers like us take on Paris.

This year, Paris will be invaded by 77 million visitors:

- 6,893,000 people will climb the Eiffel Tower. In peak season, July and August, it can take three hours to reach the top.
- 7.7 million people will schlep through the Louvre to see the Mona Lisa. The painting is only 21 inches wide and can, realistically, only be viewed by one person at a time. Prepare to wait, and wait, and wait for your turn.
- 108 people a minute will drag their feet through Notre Dame. The wear and tear of all those footsteps is cutting deep grooves into the ancient stone floors.

Yes, James and I are tourists. But not *those* kinds of tourists. We are post-modern tourists. In Paris, that means that we are *flâneurs*.

Flâneur, noun, French: one who has perfected the art of nonchalance.

Flâneurs are found in abundance in Paris, lolling in its scenic cafés and strolling aimlessly along its beautiful boulevards. They are those happy few who can make **doing nothing** look like an honorable activity. That's what James and I want to do in Paris: leave the ancient monuments alone, stay far away from the famous museums, avoid crowds, try our best to blend in with world champion *flâneurs*.

What follows is the diary of our typical *flâneur-style* day in Paris.

Le Matin
Morning in Paris

Time: 7:07 AM (dawn).
Place: 7eme arrondissement (near the Eiffel Tower).
Temp.: 65° and sunny. September in Paris is usually cool and rainy, but the city is enjoying an unusually long and fine Summer this year.

Paris doesn't do breakfast. The French think so little of breakfast that they don't even have a word for it. They call it *le petit déjeuner* which means *little lunch.* What most French people eat for their morning meal is merely a snack: a piece of fruit, a bite of pastry, a few gulps of espresso.

However, there are still a small number of people -- about five percent of the French population -- who honor the old custom of starting the day with a glass of wine, in a ritual that is called *tuer le ver;* killing the worm.

This **worm** is a legendary deadly **heartworm** (although some say that it lives in the intestines) that plagues the French. The only way to kill this deadly worm is with **a dose of wine.** So, for a long and healthy life, it is only **wise** to take the precaution of drinking a medicinal amount of booze each morning. *À votre santé.*

Choosing the right spot, the right café where we can **kill the worm** will be one of the most important decisions that James and I will make in Paris.

By my third morning in Paris I am a regular at the **Café du Marché**. I'm having my first cup of tea of the day when an old lady, another regular, arrives. She shuffles past the *patron* at the bar and picks up a small dog, asleep in a basket behind the counter. She gives him a kiss, and carries him to a corner table where she will sit with the dog on her lap, sipping her tiny cup of *café express*. Tough *mecs* (they look like butchers, or plumbers) standing at the bar with their pony glasses of *eau de vie* complain that *oh là là*, things are not *correct* these days. Two young women dressed for office work stop for a quick chat, all flusters and gestures, and when they finish their *café* they kiss each other, once, twice, four times, and, breathless and self-important, wave to each other, *"Ciao, ciao, à bientôt!"*

Overheard at the café:

A Canadian couple, slumping against each other for support, wearily stirring their espressos.

He says, "We have to budget our money better -- that breakfast cost us $200.00."

She answers, "The problem is that the kids want to try one of everything."

"We also have to stop letting them be in charge of reading the maps," he grouses.

"Well, I deserve a pat on the head for not going on about **that**," she says. There is a tired pause.

He says, "It would be a totally different trip without the kids."

"I need exactly 12 sips of wine to get my day started," a sunburnt woman in her 40s announces to her friend.

The park on the Quai d'Orsay is where we find ourselves sitting in the shade after a mile's stroll, watching the people who pass us by.

"That's us in 20 years," we say approvingly about a handsome older couple.

"That's us 20 years ago," we sigh, about a lovely bohemian twosome who are actually much too chic--and too young, to be us 20 years ago: 20 years ago I was almost 30. It's easy to forget how the years add up, between one's trips to Paris. I was a teenager the first time I sat alongside the Seine like this, and part of me is always that teenager whenever I come back. I have a feeling that Paris does this to all her visitors.

The beagle rolling in the grass, celebrating being a lucky dog who lives in Paris, is named Benedict. "Oh, yes, he is a happy dog," his owner tells me; "Not very intelligent, but very, very happy." **Travel Tip:** Ask Parisians about their dogs--it's the only time they will gladly talk to you.

The morning has become quite hot so James decides to change out of his jeans. He's got a pair of shorts in his day pack. So there he is, sitting in his underpants on a park bench on the Quai d'Orsay. Until this moment I had not known that I'd married a man who could take off his pants in public, in Paris. But learning new things about your spouse is what honeymoons are for, *non?*

Tips About What to Wear in Paris

Beware those whiny expats who complain that we, their fellow citizens, embarrass them when we visit Paris wearing our khaki pants and baseball caps.

Since when did "looking American" become such a huge *faux pas?*

Americans who live in Paris suffer from too much contact with Parisians, who are all maniacally conformist. Why should you, the footloose wanderer abroad, a paying stranger in a land that welcomes paying strangers, care whether or not your vestments are *de rigueur?*

The answer is: you shouldn't. Trust me. I used to be an expat here, I used to whine about Californians in jogging pants on the Champs Elysées and Floridians in Bermuda shorts in the Louvre. Then I married a man of true *savoir vivre*, and he's wearing his souvenir 2001 World Series cap up and down the *grands boulevards.*

Yes, it is true that the better you are dressed in Paris, the better you will be treated. But that is because Paris is not New York, where I trained as a concierge at a five-star hotel on Fifth Avenue and was ordered by management to **never** judge a guest by his clothes. In America, the billionaire VIP could very well be wearing a T-shirt and shabby shoes.

A Frenchwoman explained her countrymen's disdain of the way we Americans dress ourselves to Edmund White, a former longtime expat in Paris:

In Paris everyone is judging everyone, and the only people who have this American style insouciance are the insane.

Three Truths: **One:** You are not Parisian and you never will be. Don't let that bother you.
Two: Parisians don't want to know you, no matter how well you dress, so you might as well be **yourself.**
Three: Deep down, Parisians are crazy jealous that they can't let loose like us crazy Americans.

I stop a passerby to ask him the meaning of a shop sign: Chat Huant. *Chat*, I know, means *cat*; but **qu'est-ce que c'est huant?** The young man answers in English, "Ees a nigh burr an' ee say *huant huant*." I get it: night bird = owl; *huant* = the sound an owl makes. Hooting Cat. I wonder how I could have considered myself fluent in French and not have known the word for hooting. And now I have two souvenirs for the day: a new French word, and an adorable new **nigh burr**.

Around the corner, I spot a **live cat**, perched on top of a parked car on a hectic Latin Quarter street. He ignores me, and bats my hand away every time I reach to pet him -- he's a **Paris** cat alright. He's getting the attention of every other passing cat lover, but he doesn't budge from his haughty perch atop his Renault throne.

An old jazz tune drifts from the open door of a café, taxi horns honk in F minor (a more interesting and sadder note than American taxis), a clarinet swings a jaunty tune in the background. This is the "walking theme" from George Gershwin's tone poem called *An American in Paris*.

"My purpose here," the composer explained, "is to portray the impressions of an American visitor in Paris as he strolls about the city, listens to the various street noises, and absorbs the French atmosphere."

That was 1928. There is less melody these days, more percussion (roaring motorcycles on the boulevards hitting all the sharp notes in the key of D), but the rhythm remains the same. Sauntering, easy, and proud.

Footloose on a fine day, we are wandering to our own **walking theme.**

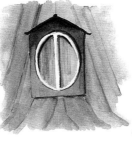

La LUCARNE
any small
window or
porthole;
also **poetic**
for: view,
outlook,
frame of mind, &
window

poet's garret,
maid's room,
foreign student
in the attic

la FENÊTRE
POUR TOITURE
Dormer Window,
invented for the
Mansard roof

novelist's
atelier

les FENÊTRES
à la
FRANÇAISE

French windows
open *inward*,
Fenêtres à l'Anglaise
(English windows)
open *outward*.

The typical sash
or double-hung
window in
America is a
FENÊTRE
à
GUILLOTINE

Diarist taking
notes on all her
neighbors for future
memoir,
homesick **au pair**
writes long letters to
school friends in
bedroom full of
DEUXIÈME EMPIRE
furniture,
bachelor existentialist
nurses a hangover

*les
fenêtres
de Paris*

Facts
and
Fictions

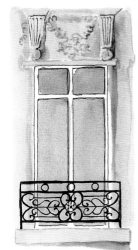

wife of billionaire
dresses for lunch
date with dear
friend Caroline
of Monaco
(Chanel suit,
Cartier tank
watch, Louboutin
flats in
burgundy
Pigalle patent-
leather)

mistress of
billionaire
dresses for lunch
date with head
of DROUOT
to discuss job
with auction
house in P.R.
Dept.

(Stella McCartney
all the way)

Remembering Princess Diana on the Pont de l'Alma

A year after Diana, Princess of Wales, died in a car crash in the tunnel under the Pont de l'Alma, the city of Paris dedicated its official memorial to her: a children's garden behind a primary school at 21, Rue des Blancs Manteaux in the Marais. This spot is, in the words of an embarrassed city councilor, "a thousand square meters of leeks," a raggedy vegetable garden, he said, an unworthy memorial for the princess.

No matter; the people who cherish the memory of Lady Diana Spencer had already chosen their monument: the **Flame of Liberty** on the Place de l'Alma, at the entrance to the highway tunnel where Diana died on August 31, 1997.

James does not get Princess Diana. (Most men don't.) I don't need a good reason for wanting to come to the Place de l'Alma to visit the people's shrine to Princess Diana. That's my philosophy of life and travel: I don't need a **good** reason. Anyway, my reasons for coming to this corner of the 8th arrondissement are murky even to me. Because I felt some connection to the princess's unhappy quest for love? Because I mourn that her life was cut short? Because I have something I need to say to her spirit? James still doesn't get it. "Those are my reasons," I tell him; "I don't need *good* reasons." (Good enough is reason enough.)

French

English

American

Question:
Which piece of street furniture here gets a mention in Proust's
À La Recherche du Temps Perdu?

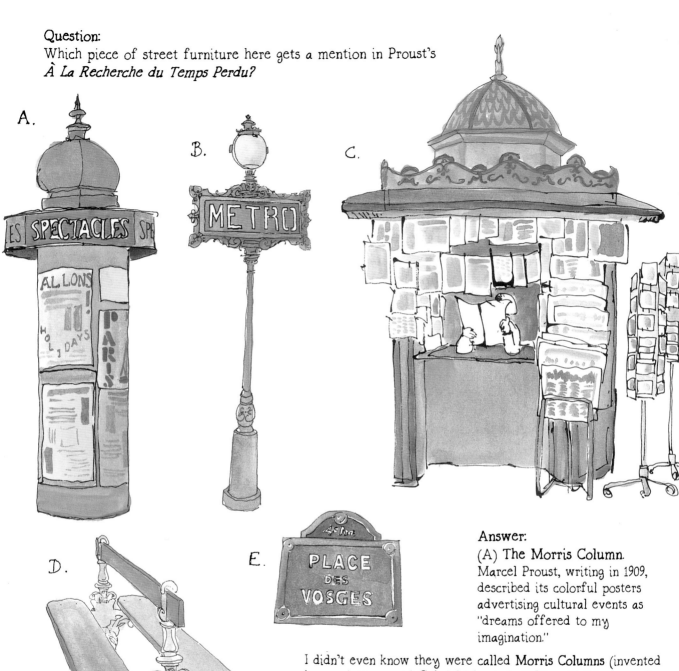

A.

B. METRO

C.

D.

E. 4ᵉ Arr. PLACE DES VOSGES

ES SPECTACLES SPE
ALLONS!
HOLIDAYS
PARIS

Answer:
(A) The Morris Column.
Marcel Proust, writing in 1909,
described its colorful posters
advertising cultural events as
"dreams offered to my
imagination."

I didn't even know they were called **Morris Columns** (invented
by a printer named Gabriel Morris in 1850) until this year. It
never occurred to me that these things had a *name*. For three
decades I've called them "Those tall round things that are always
in bad paintings of Paris -- you know! Those big tube things with
the domes on top! The pillar-like street-corner things! Green,
kind of blue-green -- you know?!"
     Knowing that they were called **Morris Columns** would
have made my life much, much easier.

26

Question:
What is the official color of Paris?

A. Gray Without Melancholy, as in the sky on a typical overcast day in the Ile-de-France.

B. The honey color of the morning sun warming up the Oise limestone exterior of the Louvre.

C. The quicksilver surface of the Seine in the wake of a *Bateau-Mouche.*

D. Mansard Blue, the color of Paris rooftops with the sound of an Edith Piaf record playing in the background.

Answer:
All of the above, plus *Vert-de-gris.*

By custom, *vert-de-gris* (a dark blue-green) was the color of Paris street furnishings such as park benches, book stalls, and water fountains.

In the early 1980s, a specific shade of *vert-de-gris* was mandated for all such public equipment in order to give harmony to the public spaces of the city.

The official shade is a mix of chrome green oxide and copper blue phthalocyanine, which results in an earthy but intense hue that is saturated with a velvety, poetic moodiness.

Vert-de-gris. This is the color that gives Paris an air of pensiveness, an introspective quality lacking, for example, in Hong Kong or Rio de Janeiro.

Asseyez-vous.
Paris Park Chairs

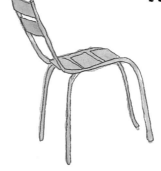

In the Champ de Mars

In the Bois de Boulogne

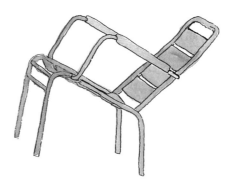

In the Jardin du Luxembourg

In the Jardin Saint-Gilles Grand Veneur

Window Shopping for Chic

A Crash Course on the Louies

Louis XIV, The Sun King (1638 - 1715). Massive and masculine, the style is characterized by tortoise shell veneer, brass inlays, heavy gilt mounts in the form of shells, satyrs, cherubs, and garlands.

Louis XV , *"Après moi, le déluge"* (1710 - 1774). Romantic, feminine, flowing, curved, and, in spite of its elaborate decorations, light and graceful. Decorative motifs include cupids, shepherdesses, musical instruments, and bouquets of flowers.

Louis XVI, husband to Marie Antoinette (1754 - 1793). Similar to Louis XV in delicacy but with simpler lines, the silhouette being straight and slim in the manner of the classical architecture of ancient Rome. Surface decoration is spare, consisting of columns and urns and other motifs from antiquity.

Chic: first used during France's Second Empire (1852 - 1870); original meaning **subtlety**, from the German **schick**: *tact, skill.*

Chic: made up by the French to make the rest of us feel dowdy; reason why the Fashion Editor of *Le Figaro* advises that nobody foreign-born should take up residence in Paris before the age of 40 so that one has had the time to establish a strong sense of self, sufficient to withstand the snotty sales girls at Hermès.

le Stiletto

Ballerina Flats

The Five Course School lunch in France.

Restauration Scolaire
These are actual menus
from a real school in France:

Moules marinières
Salade d'endive aux noix
Longe de porc au four
Brunoise de légumes
Éclair

Céleri rémoulade
Goulash de boeuf
Filet de colin pané
Petits pois carottes
Magdelena à chocolate

Macédoine mayonnaise
Boeuf bourguignon
Chou-fleur a la béchamel
Camembert
Gaufre pâtissière au sucre

Le Midi
Time for Lunch

This would never happen in America.

We would *never* be offered a "very beautiful lettuce" at our corner grocery store. But in Paris, when James inspects the produce for his lunchtime veggies, the merchant shows him a special head of *Craquerelle du Midi* and says, with a straight face, "*Voilà, c'est une très belle salade, monsieur.*"

James is certainly the kind of guy who can appreciate a very beautiful lettuce. He likes to eat his vegetables raw and the fact that the French have a special word for veggies that are eaten raw -- *crudité* -- shows that they, too, take these things seriously.

But that's just the beginning of our quest for the picnic lunch in Paris. We have still a five-course shopping *courses* ahead.

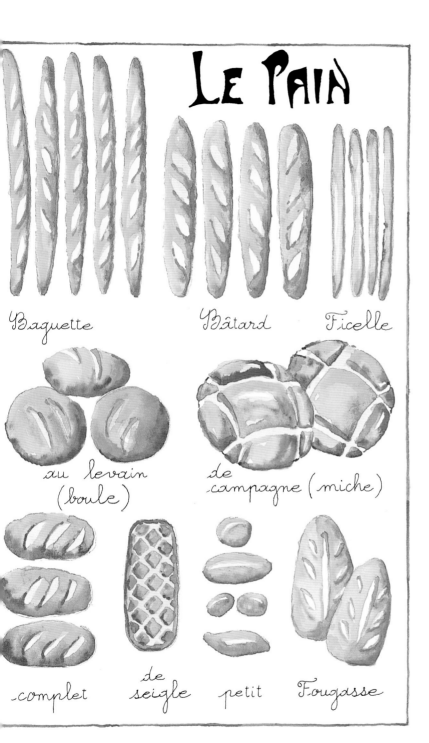

Le Pain

Baguette   Bâtard   Ficelle

au levain
(boule)

de
campagne (miche)

complet   de
seigle   petit   Fougasse

First course:
La Boulangerie

The French famously have no word for **home**. And why should they? When they have *boulangeries?*

The smell of baking bread is the very essence of hominess. And when the *boulanger* keeps his stoves fired all day long, there's always a glowing hearth to warm you, even on a Summer day.

Enter the shop and you're greeted with a kindly "*Bonjour, Madame*," a sing-song welcome just for you.

The trays of croissants still hot from the oven, the well-worn wicker bread baskets, the carefully arrayed paper doilies. It's as if your own grandmother was in charge of the decor.

And then there's your choice of any number of treats according to the mood of the day. Maybe something sweet like a *pain au chocolat*, maybe something savory like an onion *fougasse* sprinkled with thyme, or a *sablé*, buttery and reassuring, a *spécialité de la maison.*

If that's not **home**, then it's **heaven**.

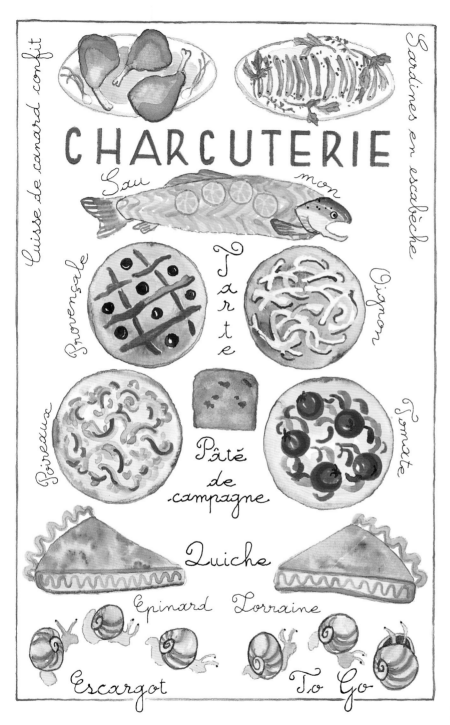

Cuisse de canard confit

Sardines en escabèche

CHARCUTERIE

Sau   mon

Tarte

Provençale

Oignon

Poireaux

Pâté
de
campagne

Tomate

Quiche

Epinard   Lorraine

Escargot   To Go

Second course:
Chez le Traiteur

James and I are blissfully compatible, but we disagree on one thing: liver.

In our everyday lives, liver is not an issue. I live for months and years at a time without liver. At home, it never crosses my mind to seek out the fancy food stores that stock imported chopped liver and, in fact, I normally avoid mushy meats altogether.

But we're in France, and France unleashes the carnivore in me. I lust after **liver pâté**.

In addition to the earthiness of the main ingredient (pig or goose liver), there is butter, cream, wine or brandy, and the classic *quatre épices*.

Quatre épices -- four spices -- is the name for the six spices that give chopped liver its gourmet credentials : pepper, coriander, nutmeg, ginger, clove, and allspice. It's alchemy the way they combine to unleash liver's latent characteristics (I taste evergreen, and sea-spray) to offer a meaty, nostalgic adventure for the taste buds.

The flavors are so much more mischievous than anything I normally tolerate. With each bite, I taste velvet dresses I've never owned, poems I should know by heart, the life I might have had if I'd been born on the Ile-de-France instead of Montana.

Ah, I just love pâté.
James hates the stuff.

Third course:
La Fromagerie

"*Monsieur*," said the *fromager* to one of his best customers, "I shall refuse to sell you my cheeses if you persist in drinking lemonade with them." *

In the life that we've left behind in America, there is nothing that comes close to the smell of a French cheese shop. I can barely stand it -- such ripe aromas -- but James, who has a much keener sense of smell than I, tells me that it is the good, deep scent of *terroir.*

He eagerly consults with the merchants who age the cheeses they sell, storing them for days or months in cold, moist cellars, sometimes even bathing the young cheeses each day in beer, salt water, or secret *eaux-de-vie.* He loves it when he's asked whether he will be eating the cheese for lunch or dinner; the *fromager* knows which of his cheeses will be just exactly right in *four*, or *eight*, hours.

After ten minutes in the company of *Brie de Meaux, Pont l'Evêque, Maroilles,* etc., I have to flee. I dash outside to the sidewalk, gulping down city air, car exhaust, and dog poop fumes, for relief.

*Reported by Anthony Glynn, about his local *fromager* on the Île St.-Louis, in his book The Seine (1966).

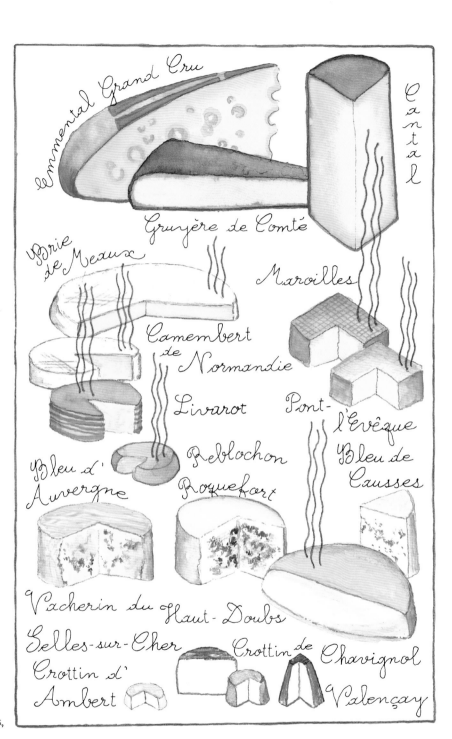

Emmental Grand Cru

Cantal

Gruyère de Comté

Brie de Meaux

Maroilles

Camembert de Normandie

Livarot

Pont-l'Evêque

Bleu d'Auvergne

Reblochon

Bleu de Causses

Roquefort

Vacherin du Haut-Doubs

Selles-sur-Cher

Crottin d'Ambert

Crottin de Chavignol

Valençay

Something Good

For Dessert

Fourth course:
La Pâtisserie

The Museum of Cravings.

The cakes are small, just right for serving a private, individual indulgence.

They are arranged in *les vitrines* that glisten like jewel cases.

Each miniature creation is a wish-sized landscape, or an intimate still life of desire.

Each name is like a French haiku.

Millefeuilles the thousand-leaf layer cake.

Gâteau opéra, an aria of coffee butter cream and dark chocolate with sponge cake for *tessitura.*

Les éclairs, the lightning without thunder (the zig-zag icing decoration gives the treat its name).

Les petits fours, the little fires, all unquenchable.

Sorry. I got a little carried away.

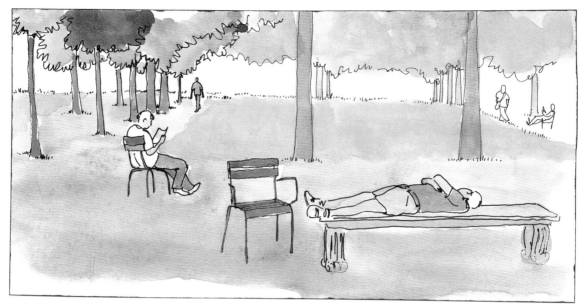

Fifth course:

Le Nap

After a picnic lunch, James stretches out on a cement
bench for his afternoon snooze. Another **Honeymoon
Lesson**: my husband can -- and will -- sleep *anywhere*.

Things I Think About While James Sleeps in the Tuileries Gardens

The guide books say that you're supposed to sit here
and "admire this garden designed by Le Nôtre for Louis
XIV. " Who *does* that? I'm looking around and I see
people sunbathing, watching their kids play, striding
through the shade in business suits, Parisians being
Parisians. I don't see anybody sitting and admiring the
landscape. Lots of people are reading. Is that guy over
there reading a *cookbook?*

Once, on a train from London to Edinburgh, I watched a
guy read Brecht. He was *very* handsome. I wish I'd said
something to him. But what on Earth do you say to a
good-looking man reading Brecht?

And then there was that guy I met while hitchhiking to
San Francisco. We went to a bookstore and he shoplifted
Jonathan Livingston Seagull because he was a communist.
We were young. We were stupid.

I remember sitting in this garden for the
first time in 1975. A student berated me for
not buying her protest magazine, for not
showing *la solidarité*. What a creep. As if I
owed her my four francs.

Wait, wait... I should think of something
philosophical here, or else this desultory
hour in **the** Tuileries will be the hour I
remember most vividly of my honeymoon in
Paris.

Think deep, **think deep**...   Jeeze. I used to
live here, used to call Paris **home** -- you'd
think I'd have a lot on my mind about being
back after a 10-year absence.

Oooh, look -- a magpie!

Découverte du Patron
Vin de Pays "Lot"
Rouge 2002
le bouteille   30,00
le verre   5,50

L'Heure Verte
The Green Hour

The Green Hour is when *flâneurs* like us hit the café, to get a good seat to watch the spectacle of life that quickens the pace of Paris in the late afternoon. There is a tradition that the hours between five and seven o'clock are set aside for *amour*, when married lovers rush to each other's embrace, when a modern Romeo meets his Juliet. It's called the **Green Hour** because The French have an unusual appreciation for the color **green**. To them, it is the color of spice, vigor, and lust -- they call a tart wine and a *risqué* story **green** and they love their randy old King Henri IV as The **Green Gallant**.

The Green Hour might also refer to the shade of the *flâneur's* favorite cocktail hour drink, the celadon-hued liquid narcotic *absinthe*. Banned in 1915 but making a comeback among nostalgic hipsters, absinthe is still a naughty memory that colors this time of day -- part Happy Hour, part Lost Weekend.

It takes some getting used to, this open-air theater and the frank interest that Parisians take in one another. The unself- conscious gaze they direct at anyone who catches their attention, the way they study a face or a cravat, a well-put-together ensemble or a beautiful coif, as if it were on display at the Louvre. Some visitors never get the hang of it:

"**A course and disgusting liberty**" is how the wonderfully cranky English tourist E. V. Lucas described this Parisian practice of **seeing and being seen**. But even he could not resist the charm of the Green Hour -- his advice:

Rejoice in the privilege of a quiet recess in which to sip an aperitif, and talk, and watch the world, and anticipate a good dinner.

E. V. Lucas (1868 - 1938)
A Wanderer in Paris (1909)

NOUS VOUS ACCUEILLONS
TOUS LES JOURS
DE
$12^H00 - 00^H30$

Soupe gratinée à l'oignon   5,50

Tartine de jour
         porc en confis   8,50

Tartine gamblas   8,50

Tomates "Maison"   9,00

Salade de l'été   9,50

Salade Nicoise   8,50

Tarte à l'oignon   9,00

Tarte brocolis-chévre   8,00

Hamburger oeuf à cheval   9,00

Steack, pommes sautées   11,50
Sauce au choix:
      Béarnaise, poivre

Entrecôte grillée, pommes sautée,
               Salade vertes
                              15,00
Assiette 3 Fromages
                              7,50

37

Overheard in the café:

"I've **always** been a seeker," a young woman says to her young man.

"I detest injustice," a serious young lady announces to a table full of other serious young people. They all nod.

"Worse than *Ishtar?*
Worse than *Waterworld?*"
      A young *cinéaste* demands to know.

"I can't worship anything that rusts, rots, or dies," explains a guy who, from the looks of his hair, doesn't worship good grooming either.

"Some people have problems on purpose, and some people have problems by accident," an old man explains to his companion (daughter? amanuensis?) "I have problems on purpose," he continues, "Ones I can fix." She says, "I have problems by accident. They're more interesting."

"I've never weighed more than 60 kilos," a thin middle-aged woman declares to her skinny friend.

This is the best place to be
if you don't own a palace in Paris.

It's late afternoon at café Les Deux Palais on the Île de la Cité. Headquarters for the whole of French history -- the ancient Parisii tribe set up camp on this very spot when the island was nothing but a mound of dirt, the Seine a muddy moat. Two blocks away, in the shadow of Notre Dame, is the very heart of Paris, Point Zéro des Routes de France. The world is a wheel and we are at its hub. We sit side by side on the worn leather banquette that runs the length of the long mirrored wall in the Art Deco bar.

The French speak softly in public places. They lean toward each other across the small cafe tables. Under murmured discussion might be the unseasonably warm weather (*merci* to all the pretty girls still wearing their Summer dresses). Maybe gossip of the latest legal drama; after all, the massive iron gates (gilt coats of arms gleaming in the warm sunshine) of the Palais de Justice are just across the street. No raucous laughter here -- no one laughs out loud at French jokes; the humor is wry, often just a play on words, a smile will do, if only with the eyes. The room seems full of whispered stories and eager, sympathetic listeners.

"So far so good," James says, lifting his glass of *vin rouge* in a toast to our honeymoon.

"To our last night in Paris," I agree, content with the day and ourselves. The wine is a St.-Emilion, a robust red with a whiff of the woods and misty meadows that we hope to discover, farther down the road, in the hills of Bordeaux.

"Our last night in Paris!" J. says, stretching, leaning back in his seat. His body language is very un-French.

"The best is yet to be," I say, not sure if I'm quoting a love poem or the one about Xanadu. Either one works for me.

Luminous Afternoon

Remembrance Blue

The 7 o'clock Colors of Paris

Secrets in the Stones

The Color of Lost Footsteps

L'Heure Bleue

On the Île Saint-Louis

In the late afternoon, wandering in
and out of the shadows.

Here is where Baudelaire squandered
his family's fortune by writing indecent
poems and hosting the Hashish-Eaters
Club. From the walls that surround this
privileged island/village we look down
on the river. A man sits on the deck of
his houseboat and reads his evening
newspaper. His boat is called
L'Heure Bleue. The Blue Hour.

The early evening sunlight scatters in
the air like gold dust, motes of *bien-être*
(almost tangible) drifting in the breeze.

It's time to wander toward dinner.

I remember my first taste of classic French food: I was 19, on my own in Paris. I pointed to a slice of *quiche Lorraine* at a charcuterie. *"Je voudrais ça, s'il vous plaît,"* I said. The delicacy was wrapped in a tissue paper packet that I carried back to my hotel room. First bite: more mushy than I expected. Second bite: a strange mix of cream and salt. Third bite: I am now a *gourmet*.

I am a gourmet was my motto by the time I came to live in Paris the year I was 22. I ate *caviar, escargot,* frogs' legs, *foie gras*, brains, and an assortment of the *abats* white and red -- stuff that I never want to eat again, now that I've given up trying to be sophisticated. It's hard for me to think of anything that interests me less, these days, than fine dining -- stories about strangers' grandchildren, maybe; or puns.

Today I'm not ashamed to admit that my favorite dish is a plain grilled cheese sandwich. Some of the greatest French chefs have tastes that are similarly simple: Jacques Pépin, when asked what he would want for his last meal, said "A good piece of bread -- and some good butter."

James's first experience of French food was frogs' legs, cooked at home, when he was seven years old. James's parents were culturally ambitious Americans who believed in French food -- his father was an adventurous eater (who knew the difference between *abat blanc* and *abat rouge* -- to you and me it's just offal) and his mother was an excellent cook. But not so excellent that she could get a seven-year-old to eat frogs' legs. To this day, J. can't stand the sight of tiny amphibian body parts on a dinner plate.

Dinner in Paris

For me: Pâté de campagne
Salade parmentière (potatoes, vinaigrette, herbs, and seasonings)
Haricots verts
Assiette de fromages
Vanilla flan

James: Mussels in a cream sauce
Warm salad with goat cheese
Grilled salmon
Mushroom gratin
Assiette de fromages
Crème brûlée

Cuisine Très Soignée Service Rapide PRIX FIXE

If you can judge a restaurant by its name then **Tango du Chat** is our kind of place.

Our waitress is young, redheaded, and *très sérieuse*. She's brought her dog to work with her, a cute wire-haired mutt with one ear that goes up and one ear that flops down. She settles the pooch behind the bar, whips her apron around her waist, and stands at attention to take our order.

"What's your dog's name?" I ask. The waitress gives me a cold look. She's trying to size me up. Dog lover, or pain-in-the-ass Board of Health type American?

"Your dog -- she's *mignon*," I assure her.

The waitress relaxes. "Effie," the girl tells me. And we both turn to look at Effie, peeking her head out from behind the bar, one ear up and one ear flopping down.

I tell James to leave a big tip.

And then we went for a twilight walk along the Seine.

43

L'Heure Bleue   The Blue Hour

Parisian Jacques Guerlain was a third-generation master perfumer when he created the fragrance he called *L'Heure Bleue* in 1912. The Blue Hour is that the time of day between sunset and twilight when the sky is illuminated with light from the upper atmosphere, giving a nostalgic, melancholy glow to the oncoming night. The perfume evokes that time of day as an aromatic mix of almonds, vanilla, and *dust* -- all carried by the lush, long-lasting scent of jasmine and *la Rose de Bulgarie.*

Le Bon Soir
Evening on the Seine

From the **Pont Mirabeau** to the **Pont de Tolbiac** there are 27 bridges in central Paris linking the left bank to the right, or the right bank to the left, depending on which side you think is more in need of **connection**. Some transport commuter traffic in and out of the more *chic* neighborhoods, some double as above-ground metro lines, some act as shortcuts for tourists trekking from one must-see landmark to another.

      The **Pont Neuf**, built like a fortress across the tip on the Île de la Cité in 1607, is the oldest bridge in Paris. **The Pont des Arts** has a graceful lacework wrought iron *passerelle* design from 1804. They face one another on the river, each a span between the intellectualism of the 6eme arrondissement and the grandeur of the 1ere; one's medieval gravitas reflecting off the other's Enlightenment tracery. These are the two bridges in Paris that take James and me where we most want to go.

A Crash Course
on the Rivers of France

The sun sets down-river on **La Seine**,
the river that the French call *sage.*

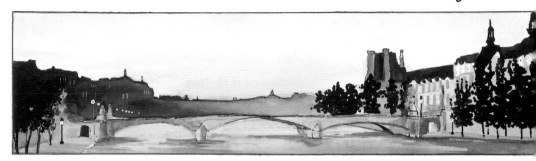

La Loire -- wayward, *capricieux*
La Garonne -- fierce, *redoutable.*
Le Rhône -- primitive, but
une puissance conquise
These four rivers are the first among
all the *rivières* of France, the four
mighty *fleuves* that flow to the sea
(all west-ward, except for the Rhône
which flows south).

When does a *rivière* (a tributary) become
a *fleuve?* In France, it's a philosophical
question, and there are some people --
mapmakers and hydrologists, not poets --
who insist that it is **not** the **Seine** but its
formidable tributary the **Yonne**. which
flows through Paris. Try pronouncing
l'Yonne, and be thankful that the normal
rules of geography don't apply here.

La Nuit

In the City of Light

Northern Lights in the City of Lights. Nine o'clock on a
September night and the sun is just now setting in the skies
above the Seine. Of course -- Paris is farther north than
Montreal, as close to the Arctic Circle as the Aleutian Islands
and Thunder Bay.

Due east along the 48th parallel there's Ulaanbaatar,
where Mongol shepherds are watching this twilight and telling
the ancient story of the Pleiades -- the Seven Sisters turned into
stars -- and their love for the handsome hunter who roams
among the constellations searching for them. I know those tribal
astronomers aren't thinking of us, here on the Pont des Arts
watching for the arrival of that same M45 star cluster, but if I
were a love-struck maiden made of stardust I can't think of any
place I'd rather be.

Postcard from the Pont des Arts

They were as unexpected as a mirage, those dancers on the Pont des Arts. Strictly speaking, the bridge is for pedestrians only, but waltzing is allowed on special nights like this. A guitar, a violin, an accordian — a tune everyone knows — and the dancers begin to twirl, spin, soar, and glide all around us, in love with life at 3/4 time.

Did I say waltzing was allowed?

Under these circumstances, it's _mandatory_.

A dance, a kiss or two under the stars, a walk through quiet streets at midnight, a good night's sleep. Tomorrow we hit the road, for **La France Profonde**.

Phase Three: The Reality Check

A little bump in the road.

The Reality Check.
A little bump in the road of love and travel.

LOVE: People in love are lousy navigators. Infatuation makes them blind, *and* dumb: research (real, scientific research) has found that the emotions associated with infatuation (bliss, foolish devotion, etc.) suppress crucial biological brain functions -- specifically, the functions of **critical thinking.**

> Love is blind and lovers cannot see
> The pretty follies that themselves commit,
> For if they could, Cupid himself would blush
> William Shakespeare, *The Merchant of Venice* (1596)

Sooner or later, **reality** worms its way into a love affair. Something little: a bad mood, a sharp word, a revealing foible (he collects broken-down waffle irons, she has way too many cats) leads to the discovery that your beloved is not **perfect.** It's eye-opening. And that's not a bad thing.

TRAVEL: At some point, early on in the journey, when you are still giddy with the excitement of finding yourself on the adventure of a lifetime, you will run smack into a little **reality.** A rude shop assistant, a vexing bureaucrat, a little stumble over the language barrier -- the discovery that all is not perfection. It's eye-opening. And that's when the **real** travel begins.

Know this before you set out: Onto every road trip a little rain must fall.

It's unavoidable, destined. **There will be rainy days on your journey.** Either real precipitation (actual raindrops on your parade) or the emotional equivalent. It's those rainy days of the soul -- the little letdowns and minor mishaps that break the spell of *traveler's infatuation* -- which you must count on so when they happen to you, you won't be caught by surprise, your trip totally ruined for not having an umbrella.

I have a confession to make. I **have** noticed something about traveling with James that is the tiniest bit irritating. Until we spent these past few days walking around Paris together, I did not know that James had **opinions** about crossing streets. Having walked alone for many years, in my own land and in a number of foreign countries, I am used to going to and fro without much thought. Walking alone, I am used to **never having a conversation** about the **why's, when's,** and **how's** of getting from one side of a road to the other.

But walking in a twosome is different. It seems to require an ungoldly amount of conversation. Because, it seems, James (my new husband) has a **strategy** for crossing roads, **and a need to teach it to me.** I did **not** know that; I did not know that my street-crossing skills were so in need of improvement. I bet we've crossed 100 streets in the course of our wanderings, and have had 200 discussions about the why's, when's, and how's of getting from **one side of the road to the other.**

Discovering your beloved's foibles: isn't that what honeymoons and road trips are for?

But I refuse to have one more discussion about triangulating our rate of ambulatory momentum with the prime transverse and the speed of on-coming traffic. From now on, when we're in a crosswalk, J. has to treat me like a stranger.

Oh, and James talks too loud. France is a very *sotto voce* country and J. has a typical American fondness for being *heard,* loud and clear.

Oh, and instead of telling me straight out what he wants, he'll put it in the form of a question: **Should we exchange money here?** (Meaning, *I'm out of euros.*) **Are you going to walk to the next Metro stop?** (Meaning, *I'm walking to the next Metro stop*). **Are you hungry?** (Meaning: *I want lunch now.*) It's nothing serious, nothing that dooms our road trip. I'm in love.

But still, it's annoying.

Road Trip Reality Checks
The little things that can make a trip a little less than perfect.

A small loss of personal property.

Dr. Samuel Johnson (author of the first dictionary of the English language) got his reality check on the first day of his tour of Mull, in Scotland, in 1773: "He was more out of humor today" (wrote his traveling companion, James Boswell), "having suffered a loss, which, though small in itself, was of some consequence to him...The loss that I allude to was that of the large oak walking stick...".

It happened to have been Dr. Johnson's *favorite* walking stick: "In return for the services it had done him, [Dr. Johnson] said this morning he would make a present of it to some museum, but he little thought he was so soon to lose it."

No wonder Dr. Johnson never much liked Scotland after that.

A little financial panic.

I was almost 30, reawakening my true French soul on a return trip to my beloved Paris. I decided to go to the Louvre, something that I, a *poseur* down to the tips of the Sorbonne-student-style scarf I'd draped around my neck, hadn't done in ages. The line into the museum was packed with tourists, and I was too busy acting French to pay close attention to the woman working at the admission window. I was all the way in the Richelieu wing when I realized that my crisp, new 100-franc note (my budget for the entire day, my meal money, and my bus fare) had been skillfully reduced by a fast-acting cashier to a few bills worth only the price of one small glass of *vin ordinaire*. Moi? *Short-changed?* At the *Louvre?*

I have not been back there since.

A surprise national holiday.

They come out of the blue, those inexplicable Bank Holidays, when a country shuts down for no apparent reason (no apparent reason, that is, to a tourist). The only thing I know about Ireland's holiday called **La Saoire i mi Lunasa** is the eight hours that I sat on a hard wooden bench in the waiting room of the bus station in Roscommon in 1985. At least I'd thought to pack needles and thread so I could pass the hours using my sewing kit to embroider a Celtic alphabet but *still*: there was *nothing* else opened in town, nowhere a homeless wanderer could go. *Nowhere*, on that sad first Monday in August.

A bad night's sleep.

Edward Lear, the famous English writer, went on a tour of Greece in 1848. Not everything went smoothly. He writes that in Thessaly, in the middle of the night, the roof of his lodgings "being slight, a restless stork put one of his legs through the crevice and could not extricate it; whereon ensued much kicking and screams, and all night long the uproar was portentous. Four very wet jackdaws also came down the chimney and hopped over me and about the room until dawn."

Do you think poor Mr. Lear had a fun day's travel after *that?*

An actual rainy day.

I never went walking on Ipanema. I only had a week in Rio de Janeiro and I was *busy*. Picnic luncheons with artists, balmy outdoor dinners with millionaires. But the famous beaches were always in the background, waiting for me, for when I could spare the time to spend an afternoon in the sun. And then it *poured* rain on my last two days in Rio. I had a *rendez-vous* in São Paolo that I had to make, and a then a stopover in Buenos Aires that I couldn't miss, and I had to leave Brazil without ever setting foot on the most famous sand in Latin America.

I have forgotten everything I ate or drank in Rio; the only thing I can still taste is my regret.

"We have to go to Bayeux,"
I said to James last Winter, when we were talking about traveling in France. We have to:

• Relive the story of the only King the English call **The Conqueror**.

• Pay homage to heroes on a great American battlefield.

• Go back in time, 900 years; and then fast forward to **modern Europe**, all by walking in and out of the shadows on a cobblestone street.

• See where we'll be living when we get serious about moving to France.

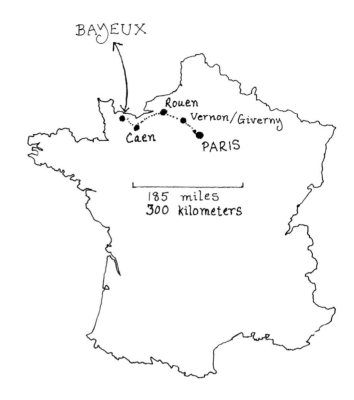

The Truth of Travel

I could write simply that
Today we traveled from Paris to Bayeux.

Or, I could specify that our journey went like this: **Paris to Bayeux, approx. 185 miles (300 km)**

1. Paris Gare St. Lazare to Vernon by commuter train
2. Vernon to Giverny and back, by bus
3. Vernon to Caen by long haul-train, changing at Rouen
4. Caen to Bayeux via rural train

Or, I could tell the truth. That our journey from Paris to Bayeux was one big tiresome reality check.

The plan was to leave Paris in the morning, make a stop at Monet's garden in Giverny, and continue on to Bayeux in Normandy. "*Non,*" the ticket agent tells me, without a glance at the schedules "It's not possible." So begins my battle with SNCF, the French national railway.

"*Mais si,*" I say; "*Regardez* [you lazy passive-aggressive little crack-pot Napoleon]: *Il y a un* train to Rouen that passes through Vernon/Giverny. And from there a train goes to Caen, then a train to Bayeux."

The ticket agent reluctantly checks his *horaires.* "*Eh bien,*" he shrugs. He allows me to pay him for our tickets and advises me that the next train to Vernon leaves in two hours. *Two hours!*

But just for the hell of it I double check: *Voilà.* There's a train to Vernon leaving in eight minutes; if I can gather up my suitcases and my husband *immediately* we have a chance of making it. We **run** like crazy people through the Gare St. Lazare to catch the train to Vernon.

Eighty minutes later we arrive at the nearly deserted town of Vernon. Deserted, except for the 50 tourists who are heading for Monet's garden with us. Local buses here are scheduled to meet each train from Paris and go directly to Giverny, a travel tip that we find out by accident once we are waved outside by the disdainful station master. We take our place at the end of a long line of foreigners standing beside an idling village bus. Nobody knows for sure that this is indeed the bus to Giverny (there isn't a sign, and the bus driver refuses to open his door to answer questions). So we wait.

At last, the driver is contractually obligated to let passengers on the bus so he begrudgingly allows everyone to scramble aboard -- and now he's annoyed that he's behind schedule. When I implore him, he says that *dommage*, there's nothing he can do about the heater that is blasting like a steam bath through the air vents on this hot Summer day. And *non*, I may **not** open a window.

Travel Tip: The French abhor drafts. They do not like the feel of the *courant d'air*, which is why they do not take it kindly when a foreigner opens a window on a train or a bus, which is probably why all the windows on the bus to Giverny were locked. Never think that, when you let in some fresh air in France, the natives won't hate you for it.

Sweating from the rolling sauna from Vernon, we are let down in a gravel parking lot some distance from Monet's house. James and I haul our wheeled suitcases with difficulty through the loose stones. After taking our money at the entrance, the staff at Giverny refuses to let us stash our luggage in their coat room. "So I'm supposed to walk through the garden dragging these suitcases?" I plead. From the way the smug manager hisses "*Oui*" at me, as if she only wishes she could make me drag a

couple of dead muskrats to boot, I know I've made her day.

So we haul our bags along another gravel path to the first flower beds in the garden, where we take a chance and leave the suitcases in an out-of-the-way corner between two restroom sheds.

Suddenly relieved of our burdens, we step lightly into the famous garden. It has been vastly renovated since my last visit 15 years ago, and I don't like the "improvements" one bit. Handrails along the walkways! Pavement where dirt paths used to be! Over ripe vegetation where meticulous flower beds once graced the lawns! Even at the lily pond, the view is obscured by an unsightly overgrowth of bamboo shoots!

And here I'd been worried that we'd have to hurry our tour of Giverny to make the 1:09 train out of town, but it turns out that we're more than ready to clear out after barely an hour here.

Our bags have remained unstolen -- our first triumph of the day -- and we straggle onto another crowded bus for the ride back to Vernon. I sit with the luggage while James dashes off to a café to get us baguette sandwiches to take with us as we continue our journey to Rouen.

Rouen: capital of Upper Normandy, site of the trial and execution of Joan of Arc in 1431.

We get off the train and check the departure boards in the station. The train to Caen leaves in an hour and a half. James wants to take a walk around the historic quarter surrounding the *gare*, see the **Place du Vieux-Marché** where St. Joan was burned at the stake, etc.

It's almost mid-afternoon and I am already tired of traveling; all I want now is a cup of tea. So I am deposited at a café as the guardian of the suitcases while James does something useful.

Giverny
A Masterpiece Garden
Home base of Impressionism

Claude Monet was on a train when he looked out the window and was entranced by the beautiful Norman countryside passing by. He moved here in 1883 and until his death in 1926 he was as much a gardener as a painter, talking to his flowers each day, greeting them by name, coaxing them to bloom and be happy.

The going rate for a Monet painting of his beloved water lilies is

$3,574.⁰⁰ per sq. centimeter

$23,319.⁰⁰ per sq. inch

Normandy

𝕎𝔲𝔩𝔡𝔬𝔯, 𝔄𝔩𝔬𝔣𝔯𝔦𝔭 𝕎𝔲𝔡𝔞𝔰!

(Thank you, King William!)

Thank you, William, Duke of Normandy, for invading England in 1066 to claim the kingdom for your own **House of Normandy**. Thank you for imposing your native language on your new subjects, who were then speaking a dialect of **old West German** (see above). Thank you for giving us our modern English language, 2/3 of which is **borrowed** from **your** Norman French.

Thank you, **Hughes d'Isigny,** for coming to England from **Normandy** with William the Conqueror. Thank you for your descendants who later emigrated to Ireland and changed the family name to **Disney**. Thank you for **Walt**, and for his **magic kingdom**, and for giving the Earl J. Wooster graduating class of 1973 the **perfect place** for our all-night party.

Travel Tip: Relax. It's not a crime to want to sit in a café and not take a walking tour of all those historic monuments in your peripheral vision.

Four teenage boys roar up to the café on their motorcycles. They take off their *casques* and shake their hair free. They gather around the table next to mine. They order Cokes and start telephoning friends, arranging for everyone to come hang out.

These boys are all so good looking, so amazingly handsome, that I have to wonder if it's because they are the Norman (Norsemen) descendants of the magnificent Vikings who settled in this part of France a thousand years ago (even though one of the boys is black), or is it because they are just too snotty to have homely friends?

One of the boys is so gorgeous that I can't take my eyes off him. When James comes to collect me even he has to admit that the kid is *beautiful*.

Back in the *gare*, I am wretched: I have misread the schedule and we have missed the 4:11 train to Caen. We have to kill 30 minutes until the next train, a slow-moving local. *Merde.*

It's on the two-hour train ride to Caen that James figures out that if we had back-tracked from Vernon/Giverny to Paris and caught an express from there, we'd have saved ourselves several hours of killing time in Rouen.

"But I would never have had that cup of tea in that café with that insanely handsome French boy," I say. (Oh, if only it were 1975 and I had been a completely different person in the past and that boy with the awesome face had glanced in my direction, if only.)

"OK, new rule,,," James says. "There are no wrong trains."

Remember, he has a degree in philosophy.

The Most Important Travel Tip of All Time: There Are No Wrong Trains.

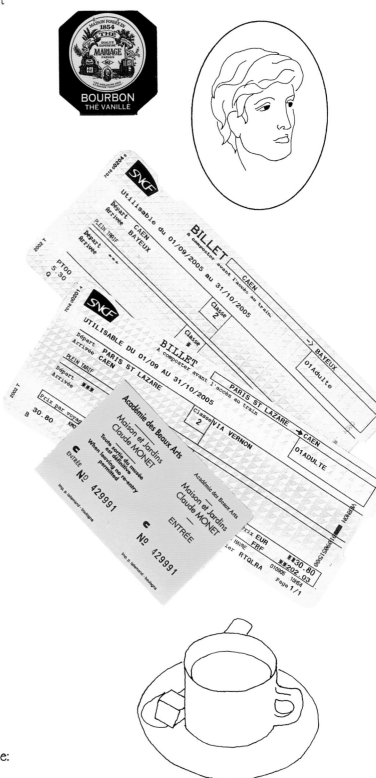

The Most Important Travel Tip of All Time:
There Are No Wrong Trains.

Panic in Caen: we have mere minutes to catch the train to Bayeux. So we claw into our pockets to find coins for the automated ticket machines on the platform, which only take exact change, if only we could figure out how they work, quickly, quickly-- luckily, the rusted old caboose to Bayeux is five minutes late and we throw ourselves on board seconds before it rolls out of the station.

We arrive in Bayeux, my favorite village in all of France, at 7:20 PM. We've been on the road for ten hours. Now all we have to do is find a hotel for the next three nights.

James is the one who enjoys scouting for the perfect hotel room, so he heads into the village while I stay behind at the train station, again the guardian of suitcases.

It is a brilliant late afternoon, the shadows long and the sunlight a deep golden wash over the quiet rail yard. Nothing is happening in Bayeux, from my point of view -- there are a few cars parked in the lot, a phone booth, an empty road, a vista of greenery in the distance, and a hotel facing the *gare*: **Hotel de la Gare**, of course. Nothing, except a light breeze, is moving. I wait, and wait. I marvel that an inhabited village can achieve such stillness, and I watch the clouds drift across a deepening sky. This might be the most alone I've ever been. Well, that's what it feels like, but not in a bad way. A cat wanders across the parking lot.

That cat is still one of my fondest memories of the day.

Or, in other words: **Today we traveled from Paris to Bayeux.**

59

Phase Four: The Honeymoon Phase

Travel at its most romantic.

The Honeymoon Phase.   Travel at its most romantic.

Love and travel. They both begin with a secret wish for a life with more adventure, more **passion**. Then you fall in love: at first, you find yourself dizzy with infatuation. Then you get some miles under your belt, some day-to-day reality. Things go wrong but *whew!* You come out alright, and **now**...

...Now, after all the planning and anticipation and the trial runs, after the delirious first steps and the little reality checks, you've finally got your bearings and here you are, at last: **travelers.** You are as different, **now**, from **ordinary people** as **peas** are from **peacocks.**

You are in a cocoon of happiness known as The Honeymoon Phase. Nothing is more **romantic.**

Romantic travel is:

- Being alive every day to new experience, bursting the confines of one's own ordinariness.
- Renewing a lost spirituality -- or searching for its meaning for the first time.
- Melding yourself into the glorious community of global humanity.
- Overdoing it a bit in the **Delusions of Grandeur** department.

Welcome, everyone, to the Honeymoon Phase of my honeymoon.

It takes time -- a few days, a few hundred miles -- for the *real* thrill of travel to kick in. You might be surprised that it doesn't happen sooner. Like, almost immediately. Like the moment you book the airplane ticket, the second you stick your thumb out for your first lift, the instant you set foot on foreign soil. But it takes a little time to not feel like an imposter, clumsily trying to inhabit this newly found freedom that fills your every day with possibilities.

It took **Sal Paradise** all the way until page 133 (almost halfway into the book) in *On The Road* for him to feel it for real:

Here we go! ...We were all delighted, we all realized we were leaving confusion and nonsense behind and performing our one and noble function of this time, *move.*

Most Romantic Travel Quote EVER:

Much have I travell'd in realms of gold, and many goodly states and kingdoms seen, round many western islands have I been...felt I like some watcher of the skies when a new planet swims into his ken; or like stout Cortez when with eagle eyes he star'd at the Pacific -- and all his men look'd at each other with wild surmise -- silent, upon a peak in Darien.

John Keats (1795 - 1821)

Least Romantic Travel Quote EVER:

I came. I saw, I conquered.

Julius Caesar (100 BCE - 44 BCE)

A Crash Course on Honeymoons

The average American honeymoon lasts eight days and takes place near a beach. How do I know this? Because the **Honeymoon Industry** ** rakes in $12 billion a year and keeps tabs on its profit centers with massive, yearly surveys.

- 99% of traditional brides and grooms go on a honeymoon.
- On average they will spend $3,700 for their romantic get away (which is triple what they would spend on any other type of vacation).
- 10 - 15% of honeymoons take place on a cruise ship.
- 75% of those honeymooners who don't want to cruise say they want to "visit a new place for sightseeing, restaurants, entertainment, and night life."
  And where will they go to find that "new place"?
    - 45% will go to a beach/lake resort
    - 20% will go to a casino
    - 10% will go on a golf course
    - 5% will go to a ski resort

Romance.   According to surveys **romance** in the **honeymoon sense of the word** means:
- Big bathtubs
- Elegant fine dining
- A "once-in-a-lifetime" trip, a place to come back from and say,
    "Guess what we did on our honeymoon!"
- Soft adventure travel, like a dude ranch
- Deluxe beds
- Shopping

** In addition to travel agents, tour operators, hospitality [hotel] providers, and airlines, the people most interested in tracking trends among the newly-wed are The Association of Bridal Consultants, The National Association of Wedding Ministers, and the Greeting Card Association.

Romance for Real.

May I say that there seems to me to be something terribly *gauche* about these honeymoon statistics? Honeymooners, and the Honeymoon Industry, tend to use the word **romance** as if it were a place on the map, a place stocked with luxury malls, hired help, and tasty snacks.   This crude idea is being branded, marketed, and sold as if ROMANCE were a **destination.**

Romance, to me, is **a state of being,** a questing, sentimental, and optimistic frame of mind that can be conjured up anywhere in the world -- Cincinnati, Fiji, or the backyard of my house on Long Island.

Romance is showing my new husband the places and things that mean the most to me.

I can't help it if some of those places and things are in France.

After Sunset in the Hudson Valley, New York

The river is frozen. James says, "Listen. You can hear the ice." Strange day (February 29th), strange sounds: the ice is a frozen-solid ebb tide, creaking and grinding in the dark.

Having spent the afternoon poking around the antiques shops in this busy little country town we came to the waterfront for a quiet rest. We have the riverbank all to ourselves.

There is something vast and spooky in the eternal darkness of a bitter cold Winter night, especially here, with this view of Storm King Mountain.

In the scheme of things, we are the most insignificant part of this landscape.

James reaches into his coat pocket and pulls out an opal ring. He kneels on the cold ground. "Will you marry me?" he asks.

I'm shivering. It's a short walk to the old inn, where we'll warm up with a pot of Darjeeling tea and make plans to elope.

This is the town of Cold Spring, Putnam County, New York. As a rule, **romance** is not a place you can find on a **map**. But sometimes it is.

Just Before Sundown in Bayeux, France

Nightingales: This part of France is the western-most Continental refuge for the legendary European thrush. We await him (only the male nightingale sings), in the Royal Botanist's garden.

The nightingale can sing two notes at the same time, a sound of heartbreak that poets have tried for two thousand years to describe. Homer called the bird's song a lament, sung only from a sacred grove of trees; *"Tender is the night,"* wrote Keats in Ode to a Nightingale. Paul Verlaine called the nightingale *mon premier amour:* My first love.

In a memory-filled forest,
under the splendor of a rising moon,
the trees' silver boughs shiver
with sorrow and joy
whenever the nightingale sings.

O, you beautiful bird --
What would a honeymoon be without a nightingale?

I was worn out by the all-day journey to Bayeux. If it had been up to me, I would have dumped our bags at the budget hotel at the railroad station on the edge of town -- I just wanted to heave myself into the nearest *auberge* with a bar. But James told me to "*hold on, you never know if there might be something special around the corner,*" so I waited while he trotted into town to investigate. Forty minutes later he reappeared with a big smile: "Wait 'till you see what I found," he said.

It's the biggest mansion in town, built by the **Royal Botanist** when he retired from Versailles (one step ahead of the French Revolutionaries). And then there's his *parc* -- the Royal Botanist, accustomed to the *plaisirs* of the Bourbon court, brought to his country estate a selection of rare trees from North America, India, and the Levant. It's here, in his well-kept wilderness, where the nightingales sing.

Songbirds in a private forest. This seems to me to be a medieval kind of luxury, more **Plantagenet** than **Eurozone**, all for only $62.00 a night.

After we check in and are shown how to use the keys in the ancient locks on the outside doors, we find ourselves at the gate to the *parc.* Atlas, the slobbering yellow Labrador who "guards" the *domain* greets us with a noticeable lack of *noblesse.* All the world over, yellow labs are all alike; just plain goofy with love for people and th treats they might have in their pockets.

Here, behind the high ston walls of the Royal Botanist's *parc,* we are secluded as if in another century. We sit in the warm shade of Indian Mahogany and Lebanon Cedars, the sun glows off the steeples of the Bayeux cathedral. It's the hour called Vespers.

The lady of the house (it feels rude to call her the "inn keeper") tells us that if we had made a reservation, there could have been champagne served to us on the terrace. Oh well. Next tim

The Royal Botanist's mansion is now a *Chambre d'Hôte,* a Bed and Breakfast for travelers like us, bumpkins from the New World. But perhaps I speak only for myself; James is not the least bit intimidated by the household treasures on display. He wanders around the *salons,* touching everything --the leather-bound books in the library, the Sèvres in the parlor. He pulls wine bottles from the cabinets and inspects their labels, he picks up *bibelots* from the mantel. "My mother used to collect jade like this," he says, checking out the *chinoiserie.*

It is a surprise to me that my husband looks at home here, as *in place* as the red velvet Louis XVI chairs and the ormolu Le Roy clock. How did I marry such a person?

Travel Tip: The term is *in situ* -- in the place of origin. We travel to put ourselves *in situ,* in a place where we *belong.* The feeling that one was born in the wrong place is an ancient and universal experience, such that I suspect (a) it is part of our human DNA; and (b) is why our kind are born wanderers. We travel to find the place where we can **recognize ourselves** for once. Be on the lookout for that jolt of unexpected familiarity in a foreign land: that's how you'll know **you** are *in situ.*

OK, I'll admit it: staying in a fancy B&B *is* romantic. I swoon, surrounded by somebody else's antiques in situ. Heirlooms, each one a memento of a privileged and epic life. Maybe those gem-stone *objets d'art* were sent by a passionate admirer of *Madame,* and this *Directoire* writing desk is where she penned her naughty thank you note.

At breakfast we meet the other paying guests, a family of five from Anchorage, Alaska. Small world: They tell me that my old high school on the south side of town was torn down last year and re-built from scratch. It was cheaper than fixing it up -- a school that was barely 35 years old. Antiques don't stand a chance in the 49th state.

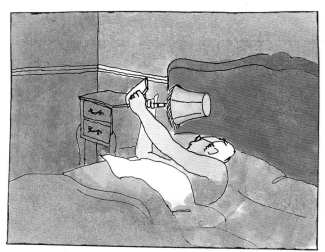

France, the land of the 20-watt light bulb. James shows his technique for reading with a typical French bedside lamp.

A travel guide popular with young backpackers describes Bayeux's municipal museum, the **Musée Baron Gérard**, as *a rather dull jumble of porcelain and lace donated by local families.*

Which is exactly true and exactly why I've been so very fond of the place since I was 20 years old. I had a precocious appreciation of banality.

I treasure back-water tourist attractions, especially if they are "museums" comprising third-rate hand-me-downs, chipped chamber pots and balding taxidermy and the like. It's not a taste shared by my husband. He wanders off towards the British War Cemetery while I investigate the museum's new acquisitions (some old locks and a few "possibly Roman" nails).

"I remember when this museum was across the street, and this place was the old lace-making school," I tell the docent who takes my admission fee. My voice sounds loud in the stillness. She and I are the only people in the building.

She seems happy for some -- *any* -- company so I stay to chat. Both of us remember this town long ago in the 1970s. In the old days, the famous **Bayeux Tapestry** was hung here, out of the way of the 20th century, in a large second-floor room that had all the charm of an old gymnasium. But then in 1983 the tapestry was relocated to a brand new spiffy stand-alone **international cultural destination**. It's there now, displayed in a scientifically darkened and climate-controlled tourist attraction down the road.

And then the lace-makers were all gone and the school was empty and they moved the museum in to fill up the echoes.

I dislike it when my favorite places are "improved".

The docent shrugs. "What can one do?" she says, *"Vous ne pouvez pas pousser contre la marée."*

You can't push against the tide.

ET · VVILLELM VENIT BAGIAS

A Crash Course on the Bayeux Tapestry

The **Bayeux Tapestry** is a Norman document executed, according to legend, by the Queen Mathilde, consort of William the Conqueror, c. 1070. This document is a 231-foot-long scroll of linen embroidery worked in worsted wool threads -- a picture story to educate an illiterate public to the rightfulness of the Norman conquest of the English people.

The **Tapestry** contains 58 scenes of travel, pilgrimage, feasts, and war in Normandy and England comprising a total of 623 men (one dwarf), 2 women, 202 horses, 55 dogs, and 505 other animals of various kinds, with 37 buildings, 41 warships, 49 trees, and one comet.

I would trade the whole Louvre for this Tapestry. I first saw the Bayeux Tapestry in photographs, when I was 10 years old, in a 1966 issue of *National Geographic* magazine that commemorated the 900th anniversary of the Norman Conquest of England.

The only thing I knew about England was the Beatles. I had never heard of *France*, let alone the *Normans*. And the only thing I knew about embroidery was the hateful cross-stitch (grandmother's gift, 8th birthday, sewing kit, forced to do it, vowed never again).

But oh! This Tapestry! This was **sewing** -- this was **art** -- on an order of magnitude that I had never imagined. And now, almost 40 years later, I can say that I learned **all** my core artistic values (craft and narrative trump concept, abstraction is a sham) from this piece of linen.

ISTI MIRANT STELLA

Halley's comet passed over the skies of France and England in March 1066. It is shown in the Tapestry as an omen, sewn as ISTI MIRANT STELLA.

THESE MEN WONDER AT THE STAR

ÆLFGYVA   TVROLD

I'm nervous about taking James to see the Bayeux Tapestry. I want my new husband to adore it as much as I do. We race past the gift shop and leg it into the gallery ahead of a bus load of elderly British tourists. Face to face with the work of art that defines **art** for me, I am excited to give James the tour, point out the best scenes, the most beautifully sewn vignettes, my favorite characters.

"Do you **love** it?" I ask James. J. says, "Sweetie, I love it that *you* love it so much." Which is pretty much the way I feel about him and the Grateful Dead. Good thing I didn't marry him in my 20s, when my idea of true love had no room for this kind of autonomy.

So he rents a bicycle for the rest of the day while I stroll the back streets of my favorite town in France. I stop in at an embroidery studio where Bayeux Tapestry sewing kits are sold.

"English bachelors are my best customers," *la propriétaire* tells me, "but the French *célibataires*, they don't sew *small* scenes -- they always want the BIG battle scenes."

I too have sewn a large portion of the Tapestry, a kit given to me by my mother 20 years ago. I used a bulky yarn that was the standard back then.

"*Alors* -- you must see the new threads!" the shop owner tells me, and together we two seamstresses inspect the new flosses, pick through the various vegetable-dyed yarns, talk about the marvelous authenticity of the fine, silk-like wool available now-a-days for a new generation of Tapestry devotees.

This counts as one of the best conversations I've ever had in my life.

NEXT LIFE

My embroidery studio on the main street of Bayeux will be just one part of my **Institute of Slow Information**. I will also teach letter writing, listening, miniature portrait painting, and the art of doing one thing at a time.

A STITCH IN TIME
EMBROIDERY STUDIO

The Bayeux Tapestry tells the story of the creation of the Anglo-Norman dynasty that changed the course of English history. So British people come to Bayeux in droves to see this b of their heritage. And what a good thing that Bayeux is the one town in France where you can count on getting an excellent cup of tea.

It's the very *best* of both worlds to sit on *terrasse* of a French tea room in the late afternoon with a cup of tea fit for an Englishman. I prefer Assam, but the whole cart looks tempting:

Les thés

Orange pekoe: ceylan, thé de cinq heures
Thé vert sur le Nil: vert citroné
Darjeeling: Himalaya, Roi des thés noirs
    Indiens
Marco Polo: thé noir fruite
Bourban: thé rouge vanille d'Afrique du sud
    (sans théine)

In 1885 **Elizabeth Wardle**, mother of fourteen and a leading member of the **Leek Embroidery Society**, decided that France wasn't the only country that deserved the **Bayeux Tapestry** S announced that "**England should have a copy o its own**" and set about gathering the materials and the workers necessary to replicate this medieval masterpiece.

She rounded up 35 like-minded gentle-women, all dedicated amateur embroiderers, ar with 100 pounds of hand-dyed wool thread and 250 yards of linen, it took them just one year sew a full-size, full-color, stitch-by-stitch repro duction of the Bayeux Tapestry (minus the naughty bits), which now hangs in the **Museum of Reading**.

Such Anglo-Saxon stamina, such over-the-to sense of mission. God, I love the Victorians.

This is the **Bayeux canal**

from the **Aure River**

that rolls into the River Vire

that flows into the **English Channel**.

As of this writing, humans have crossed
The English Channel by
> Hot air balloon
> Paddle steamer
> Breast stroke
> Heavier-than-air craft
> Solo hovercraft
> Human-powered aircraft
> Amphibious automobiles
> Hydrofoil car
> Water skis
> A bouquet of helium-filled balloons

The **Spanish Armada** (in 1588) and **Napoléon Bonaparte** (1803 - 1814) couldn't do it. Only two invading armies have ever successfully crossed the English Channel.

①The army of William, Duke of Normandy, on September 28, 1066. His 5,000 soldiers defeated the Saxon king's forces and created an Anglo-French dynasty whose descendants are still in power today.

②On June 6, 1944, the Allied armies of the United States, Great Britain, and Canada (with troops from Austria, Belgium, Czechoslovakia, Greece, the Netherlands, New Zealand, Norway, and Poland) invaded Normandy in the largest movement of men and matériel in history known as **Operation Overlord**.

Notes
at the end of the day

The tourist office closes at 6, the museums turn off their lights at 7.

The tour buses pull out of town, the day trippers from Paris head for the train station, the British holiday makers head for the Chunnel.

The souvenir shops pull down their shutters.

The roads empty, the sidewalks clear, the background noise: silence.

This is when the 20-something-year-old backpackers at the youth hostel start to complain that there is nothing to do at night in Bayeux.

Perfect.

It is 9:15 and almost dark. The sunset is a gothic concoction of pink and indigo.

How is it that, at the only restaurant with this bewitching view of the cathedral, we are the only customers? *Moules* for James, a pizza with a fried egg *à cheval* for me.

On the other side of the empty street a young couple passes by, walking hand in hand. In the faint street light I see the figure of a cat, an orange tabby, padding down the road, a few steps behind them.

We are debating whether apple brandy or Chambord would make a better nightcap when here comes the same couple, returning from their stroll; followed by the same orange tabby cat.

I have a question for the *patron*. He tells me, "*Ah oui*, Yes, I know that cat. His owners take him for a walk every night."

Me
and the cosmos.

The hedgerows of Normandy

They don't look **deadly**, especially not now, 60 years after the Battle of Normandy. Since Roman times farmers here have used these earth works -- massive **mounds**, 3 to 5 feet high, up to 10 feet wide, covered with small trees and dense scrub brush -- as the boundaries between their pastures and fields. Called **hedgerows**, thousands of these towering embankments gave Hitler's occupying army the best defensive terrain in Europe, a lethal advantage over the American First Army fighting its way off the D-Day beaches.

Notes from **A Pocket Guide to France**, prepared by the Information Branch of the Army Service Forces, United States Army, 1944 and distributed to the soldiers, sailors, and airmen who took part in the invasion and liberation of France in World War II:

You will soon discover for yourself that the French have what might be called a national character. It is made up of a half dozen outstanding characteristics:

1. The French are mentally quick.
2. Rich or poor, they are economical. Ever since the Nazis took over, thousands of French families have kept themselves alive on their modest savings.
3. The French are what they themselves call realistic. It's what we call having hard common sense.
4. The French of all classes have respect for the traditionally important values in the life of civilized man. They have respect for religion and artistic ideas. They have an extreme respect for property, whether public or private.
5. The French are individualists: stay out of local discussions, even if you have had French II in High School. In any French argument concerning internal French affairs, you will either be drowned out or find yourself involved in a first class French row.
6. The French are good talkers and magnificent cooks. Like most good talkers the French are polite. The courtesy words ("please" – "thank you", etc.) are the first things French children are taught.

James with John, George, Paul, and Ringo.

James Alexander Molloy, the son of Scottish immigrants, was born in New York City in 1911. He was 5 years old when he was orphaned and sent to the Saint Joseph's Home for Boys in Brooklyn. After six years, charity funds were raised to put him on a boat back to live with his maternal grandmother in Glasgow, Scotland, in 1922.

Twenty years later, James reclaimed his American identity when the United States declared war against Hitler and American troops began pouring into the UK through the port of Greenoch, Scotland. It took him six months, but he fought through the red tape and on March 11, 1943, James Molloy was permitted to enlist with the 29th Division of the United States Army, the fabled "Blue and Grey" regiment training in England to lead the invasion of Europe in Operation Overlord. He was 32 years old, and thanks to an Army clerk's misspelling, James Molloy became James **Malloy**.

On D-Day the 29ers were the first to hit Omaha Beach, James Malloy going in with the 175th Infantry on the third wave at 12:30 on June 7, 1944. Advancing towards St-Lô the 175th battled a vicious German counter-attack for ten days and were within 600 yards of their objective, Hill 108 -- Purple Heart Hill -- when James Malloy was shot through the heart by a German sniper.

James Malloy's Scottish-born widow and 14-year-old son, left behind in Glasgow, were sponsored by comrades in the 29th Division for emigration to New York, where they started new lives as Americans in 1946. His son, Joseph Molloy, is a proud veteran of the Korean War and lives on Long Island. He is my neighbor.

James Alexander Malloy
April 13, 1911 - June 16, 1944

I just think you should know his name.

A Pocket Guide to France

Travel Tips for American Servicemen in France, 1944

We are friends of the French and they are friends of ours.

Keep a close mouth. No bragging about anything.

No belittling either. Be generous; it won't hurt.

You are a member of the best dressed, best fed, best equipped liberating army now on earth. You are going in among the people of a former Ally of your country. They are still your kind of people who happen to speak democracy in a different language.

Americans around French men, let us remember our likenesses, not our differences. The Nazi slogan for destroying us both was "Divide and Conquer." Our American answer is "In Union There Is Strength."

The Landscape of Awe

THE ALLIED FORCES LANDING ON THIS SHORE
WHICH THEY CALL OMAHA BEACH
LIBERATED EUROPE
JUNE 6, 1944

How many tides have come and gone on this coast? is what we stand here and think. And what kind of hell was washed in with the blood-soaked waves that June morning? "The turbid ebb and flow of human misery," wrote Matthew Arnold, looking into this same body of water in 1851 and seeing in the vast, uncaring sea the smallness of human history. In the crashing waves he heard "The eternal note of sadness.," -- and we hear it, too. These waves break on sacred ground.

The Normandy American Cemetery at Omaha Beach

THIS EMBATTLED SHORE, PORTAL OF FREEDOM,
IS FOREVER HALLOWED BY THE IDEALS,
THE VALOR, AND THE SACRIFICES
OF OUR FELLOW COUNTRYMEN.

These sons of America who came to us and remained here so became, also, our sons, said the Bishop of St-Lô, in a memorial service in 1994 on the 50th anniversary of D-Day.

Block J, Row 24, Grave 23. The marble is from Italy, and like all the other 9,386 headstones of those killed in the Battle of Normandy, his faces west toward America: **James Alexander Malloy,** PFC, 175th Inf., 29th Division: the only Scottish soldier buried in the Normandy American Cemetery on Omaha Beach.

There are 26 World War II military cemeteries in Normandy:

16 British   1 Polish
2 Canadian   1 French
2 American 4 German

The memorial at the British Bayeux War Cemetery is engraved:

NOS A GULIELMO VICTI VICTORIS

PATRIAM LIBERAVIMUS

We, once conquered by William,
have now set free the Conqueror's native land

The elusive sense of history.

There were five other people waiting with us on Omaha Beach for the bus back to Bayeux, a family of four from Oklahoma (Mom, Dad, two teenage boys, all very large) and a lone backpacker from Canada. The Oklahomans tell us about their family's two-week driving tour of Europe: "Drove from Rome to Lourdes in one day. But here, we're taking a day off from the car -- that's why we're waiting for the bus." They leave Normandy tomorrow to spend a day in Paris before they catch their flight home. I ask what else they've seen in France. "Mostly Catholic shrines," they tell me.

      The Canadian says he's only spending a day in Paris, too; there are only two things he wants to see there, the Louvre and Jim Morrison's grave. He doesn't look that much older than the teenagers from Oklahoma. "You can't be old enough to know about the Lizard King!" I exclaim. "I listen to classic rock," he says.

      The Oklahomans ask, "Who's Jim Morrison?"

Time to pack up our things,
say *au revoir* to Bayeux.
I've been looking forward to this next stop,
a very special weekend -- in **Pontorson!**

Things to do while waiting for a train.

When I have to wait for a train, I amuse myself by scribbling down a list of the collective words in which our language is so rich, e.g., a pack of hounds, a shoal of fish, a peal of bells. There are about a hundred of them, but I can seldom think of more than fifty or sixty.

Frank Tatchell, *The Happy Traveller* (1923)

Train Station Meditation:
1. Sit or stand, and relax.
2. Be aware that you are **waiting for a train**.
3. Pay attention to your **waiting for a train** experience.
4. Pay no attention to your spouse, who is drinking cider from the bottle and eating a tomato and having a much better **waiting for a train** experience than you.

Blend In. On our first date, James told me that what he wanted most in the world was **an alias**. Every now and then he updates me on his latest *whims de pseudonyms*, which now include some Norman-French contenders: Erwan, Manon, Lucas, Theo (the most popular boys' names in this province), Eyire, Clovis, Rou, and Adalrik (not so popular). Voilà: the perfect *nom Normand:* Tancrède Enguerrand Guillaume.

Argue About Money.
When J. informs me that we have 80 euros in cash to last the week end, I begin to fret. James and I never fight about *anything*. We have compatible values and are old enough to tolerate differences of opinion without shouting. But he wanted to be in charge of the money and he only changes $200 at a time, as if limiting our ready cash will somehow make things cost less. I tell James that it's an uncomfortable fact of travel that the hidden costs of living at home become **everyday expenses** on the road. "You better hope there's a bank open in Pontorson," I warn him.

Travelers are encouraged to pass Pontorson by.
"**Nothing** much about **Pontorson** itself is worth **staying for**"
are the exact words of one of the most popular guide books for English-speaking tourists

Pontorson is not famous for anything, except for being the biggest town (pop. 4,107) closest to the famous cathedral of Mont St.-Michel (4 miles, 6 km away). But even as a way-station to one of the Marvels of the World, Pontorson does not lure many of the Mont's 3 million visitors a year to stick around for a romantic weekend. And that's the best reason to come here: Pontorson is as close as you can get in France to escaping the ubiquitous tourist industry infra-structure. For three decades I've wanted to come back here and savor the town the same way I did when I first saw it, as a love-struck wanderer (in love, that is, with being young and set loose in the world). **You can't go home again**, is the famous saying; I wonder if you can go back to Pontorson?

Pontorson **Pont** means **bridge** and **Orson** is the name of the chap who built the bridge in 1031. Orson's bridge spans the Couesnon River that flows on the edge of town, the traditional boundary between the provinces of Normandy and Brittany. In his pre-King of England days, William the Conqueror journeyed to Pontorson to survey the far edge of his dukedom -- his adventures here are depicted in The Bayeux Tapestry. Not too bad for a backwater town.

My youth steeped me in an opiate of boredom sufficient for the remainder of my days.

Gustave Flaubert at age 29, about his motives for writing **Madame Bovary**, his classic novel about the tedium of provincial Norman life.

Born in Rouen in **Haute Normandie** in 1821, Flaubert was, by the age of *nine*, already complaining about living in hick country, being surrounded by the stupidity of his parents' provincial friends -- and writing it all down. At 20 he drafted an autobiographical novel and called it *Novembre,* after the most barren and lonely month of the year. At age 22, he wrote to a friend: "I loathe it, I despise it. Oh, Attila, when wilt thou return, kind humanitarian, with 400,000 horsemen, to set fire to this land of trouser straps and suspenders?" At 25 he was still moaning about living a "backwater" life: "Oh, if you knew the desire, the need I feel to pack up and go far away, far from everything here that surrounds me, everything that oppresses me!"

I was a Flaubert of the American suburbs when I was in my early 20s. I too wanted escape, adventure, freedom from my dull life and the mediocre culture that surrounded me. Not trouser snaps and suspenders; platform shoes and Farrah Fawcett haircuts.

I went to France, to Gustave's back yard. And I fell in love with the very ordinariness of Normandy, which seemed deliciously *nec plus ultra-* mundane to me.

Pontorson The First Time.

July 12, 1976
Day 58, half-way through my Summer-long hitch-hike tour de France.

I had not packed a sketch book, and hadn't felt the urge to draw anything I'd seen so far. I only had some lined letter paper and a ball point pen.

I was 20 years old.

Here is Laundry Day in my $5 hotel room in Pontorson, a portrait of my independence, my wanderer's savvy, my romantic new life. This is a portrait of my first honeymoon, with myself.

This is the only picture I drew that whole Summer.

Laundry Day in Normandy.

There's a fortune of **Authentic Vintage French Linen Tea Towels** on every clothes line. These are the exact kind of linens that specialty shops in America sell for top dollar to affluent customers who pay dearly to add that touch of French Farmhouse Fabulousness to their million-dollar McMansions.

Flaubert is *so* wrong.
Even **wash day** in Normandy is achingly chic.

Normandy is the largest area in France which does not produce wine. Instead of vineyards, there are apple orchards. *Calvados* is Normandy's world-famous apple brandy and *Cidre* is its fermented apple juice, often served in tea cups. And then there's Camembert, the French National Cheese:

Camembert, poetry, bouquet of our meals; What would become of life, if you did not exist?   Jean Anthelme Brillat- Savarin (1755-1826), famous gastronome and philosopher

Camembert

HIC FECERVN: PRANDIVM : MINISTRI · ET · VINO

The Three **C**s of Normandy

Saturday Night in Pontorson

First, the aperitif, *Kir Normand* --the local variation of the French national *kir* cocktail, made here with an extra dash of Calvados and ice cold cider instead of white wine. And then, The Lone Rider. Up and down the Rue de Couesnon he zooms, riding his motorbike into the empty night, back and forth from one end of town to the other. "I know the feeling," I tell James, who has not yet heard my stories about being 17 and in my senior year of high school, driving my old Ford Galaxie 500 through Reno, Nevada, on Saturday nights, looking for something to do.

Dragging Main, we called it in 1973, up and down Virginia Street, under the arch with the town motto: **Reno: The Biggest Little City in the World,** a little city so full of so many Lone Riders. My husband was more of an **Easy Rider** back then, in the early '70s, in New Orleans on his Honda 450cc, and to hear him tell it, Saturday nights were full of pretty girls and parties in the French Quarter. What would he know about being this French kid, my Norman alter ego, dragging his heart up and down this lonely street, riding out his [our] once-and-future-perfect *raison d'être.*

Sunday in Pontorson

Sidewalk café breakfast. Then we walk to *la papeterie* to pick up the news paper, *Ouest-France*. We sit on a park bench, read. Page after page, the paper is full of stories about people absorbed in their lives, their **West France** lives -- as if this is where **real life** happens, as if our being here or not hardly matters. As if my life in America is the hypothetical one.

I go back to the hotel room, re-strategize the wardrobe, sort and fold changes of clothes, isolate dirty socks, etc., in various plastic bags to keep cooties off the clean stuff. I scoff at people who claim that travel is "broadening". Look at me, absorbed in re-packing my suitcase, sorting clothes, folding socks.

But this is nice, concentrating on where I am and what I need to do right now, in the world, *here*. I'm just taking one thing at a time, breakfast, errands, housekeeping. Keeping it all in the present moment. On second thought, maybe **that's** the secret of travel. On third thought, maybe that's the definition of happiness. I want a nap.

James is out on his own journeys for the day. I wake up and go for a walk, mosey down the road. I go to the only shop open for business (the newsstand, again), take my time buying post cards. I walk to the far side of town, meander through silent neighborhoods, take photos of houses and gardens, of the only palm tree in *Basse Normandie*. It's getting chilly so I head back to the hotel to get a sweater, then to the cafe for tea. I write postcards, catch up on my journal, decide against having a glass of wine. For now.

Months later, when it's cold and rainy (the wettest Winter on record on Long Island), I will spend an afternoon painting these pictures of the bricks and stones I saw that day. I'll be lost in thought, a traveler in my memories. I will forget my Long Island problems, remembering how it was that Sunday in Pontorson. I will be, as the French say, *contente.*

Dinner at the only restaurant open on a Sunday evening -- good thing I consider French pizza a delicacy. James, who refuses to eat in France what he can easily get at home, gets a fancy artichoke salad. At the next table sit two old men, weather-worn and stout, sharing some *vin rouge*. One of them is wearing a Johnny Hallyday T-shirt. Now is a good time for me to tell James of my love for Johnny Hallyday, the French Elvis, and the side trip that we must take in homage to the great man when we get to Bordeaux wine country.

James tells me about his day. He followed a crowd to the **Stade et Complexe Sportif Pontorson** and watched the local soccer team rally from being behind 2 - 1 to play overtime and win. The stands were packed. No wonder the town was so quiet this afternoon. Everybody was at the game.

HIC: FLVMEN: COSNONIS

After dinner, we cross the road to Orson's bridge. The sun is setting over the Couesnon River, boys are playing on its muddy banks. I get grandiose thoughts about rivers and history. How many thousands of Sundays have there been in Pontorson with boys like these rough-housing on this same riverbank, boys like young William the Conqueror? Will it be like this in America a thousand years from now, when my nation has a history as long as France's -- will its quiet Sunday towns echo with the presence of legends? I wish I could live forever.

Side Trip. We do not pretend to be Canadians, as is the fashion of Americans abroad in 2005. *"Etats-Unis?"* the driver of the jeep asks, after pulling over for us on the road to Mont St.-Michel. *"Oui,"* we admit, having prepared for this: *"Mais on n'a pas voté pour George Bush."* Our driver waves our apologies aside. *"Oh, ça, ça c'est* just politics -- we like Americans!" he says, and quizzes us on how much we are enjoying our travels in his country. "We adore France," we say. "What great weather!" This makes him proud: "It's ten degrees hotter than normal!" he boasts, speaking in Celsius. I loathe Celsius and I've always refused to learn it. But ten degrees is probably a lot. Global warming, and all.

Mont Saint-Michel is a thousand-year old monastery built on top of a granite mountain in the middle of a plain of **quicksand** off the Normandy coast. **Quicksand**, the old horror movie stand-by. Even the **Bayeux Tapestry** can't resist the quicksand: Scene 17, the Duke of Normandy at the Mont St-Michel, surrounded by the stuff -- this is the scene that's been creeping out the kids for **centuries**.

Mont St-Michel is the second-most popular tourist site in France (after the Eiffel Tower). And today, it seems as if all 3 million of the Mont's annual visitors have dropped by. But it's not just the crowds that make us ready to quit the place after an hour. Only 43 people actually *live* here: the contrast, in serenity and authenticity, between this tourist attraction and Pontorson is appalling.

One redeeming feature: I count 25 dogs on the Mont. Europeans travel (even to holy places!) **with their dogs.** A German pooch named Timmy gives me kisses when I chat with his owners, who tell me Timmy lives with 4 cats in Tubingen. The age-old question: what does **travel** look like to a **dog?** Moving pictures? A series of rooms? Reincarnation?

James says that the grapes he brought with him from Pontorson are the best grapes he's ever tasted. "Take my picture with the best grapes I've ever tasted!" he says.

I do not think it is romantic to have a picnic hanging off the ramparts of Mont St-Michel. I think it is **stupid**.

Yes, I know this makes me sound like an old worry-wart. But the older I get the more I understand that life, and love, and care-free Summer days are against all odds.

People should take better care of them.

In the end, our weekend in Pontorson cost 140 euros. Enough with keeping our money supply just one day ahead of expenses. As soon as we get to **Saint-Malo**, I'm going to insist that we go to the bank and get a big wad of cash so we don't have to keep checking our stash everyday.

Last stop on the honeymoon trail.

> There can be nothing so odd, and, at the same time, so stern and warlike, as the
> appearance presented by Saint Malo. It is a rock bristled over with walls
> and fortifications, ...all the rest is stone hewn and unhewn; and a more bare,
> threatening and military *tout ensemble* it is not possible to conceive.
> Leitch Ritchie, *Travelling Sketches on the Sea-Coast of France* (1834)

Saint-Malo is a walled city off the coast of Brittany. It is surrounded on all sides by the English Channel, called here the *Mor-Breizh*, the Brittany Sea. Tides on this coast are deadly -- the highest and swiftest in Europe -- and warning signs posted on the beach alert visitors to beware that the incoming waters can overtake a man at the pace of a galloping horse. And then there are the mermaids lurking offshore, casting spells on sailors and ships to drag them down to their underwater palaces. The people of this province are converts to the Celtic -- not **Roman** -- brand of Christianity (the founder of Saint-Malo was the Welsh missionary **Maclou**, in 550 AD) and belief in wicked sea sprites is just part of the ancient *vie marine*. Not to mention Saint-Malo's proud history of being home to the richest pirates of the 16th and 17th centuries -- there is no place as **outlaw** and **whimsical** as Saint-Malo, which still thinks of itself as a self-governing fortress only incidentally mapped as part of France. Like they say:

Ni Français, ni Breton, Malouin suis, Malouin je reste.

Neither French, nor Breton, I am of Saint-Malo and of Saint-Malo I will forever be.

> The Malouin spirit of independence makes the people
> the most disagreeable shopkeepers in Europe.
> Leitch Ritchie, again (see above)

All morning there had been a light rain as our bus slowly made its way down narrow back roads to Saint-Malo, picking up house wives in one-house hamlets for their shopping trips into town. An elderly *femme de charge* sits with us, delighted to be our tour guide. She tells us that the cauliflower of Brittany is just as *merveilleux* as its world-famous oysters. The bus driver makes an illegal turn into the bus terminal, muttering to himself, *"Pas bien, pas bien, pas bien."*

Our hotel is in the heart of the old city. Our room on the third floor has a view of the courtyard of the adjacent apartment buildings. I look out the window and I freeze with fear. There's a kitten, about to lose one of its nine lives, walking on the clothes line hanging outside an open window. I can't breathe until I see him wobble back to the safety of the sill.

We climb up onto the ramparts to get our first tour of the city. Only 1½ miles long (2 km), the journey atop the stone wall that surrounds Saint-Malo takes two hours because there's too much to see in every direction, too many opportunities to stop, stare, and wonder why the hell we've wasted our lives not living in Saint-Malo.

The Riddle of Saint-Malo

A wooden boat departs Brittany for a voyage around the world. At each port of call, repairs to the boat are made--rotted planks are replaced with new boards, damage is patched over, missing bits are recreated. By the time the boat has circumnavigated the Earth, every plank, mast, fitting has been replaced.

Is it still the same boat?

Saint-Malo burned down in 1661. The city was built anew, in the latest style, under the care of the master architect of the age, the **Maréchal de France Marquis de Vauban.** Saint-Malo then became a show piece of Vauban's highly refined defensive style, medieval in function as a highly-fortified citadel, but wholly Enlightenment in its allowances for domestic human activities in gracious public spaces and commodious private *appartements.*

During World War II, 80% of Saint-Malo was destroyed by Allied bombers targeting its Nazi occupiers. After the war, the Malouins vowed to preserve their city's distinctive architectural integrity and they rebuilt it, stone by stone, in its precise 1661 image.

Is it still the same boat?

Three fortified islands form the first line of defense for Saint-Malo against attack by sea. The largest island, called the **Grand Bé**, is also the tomb of the Romantic writer **François-René de Chateaubriand** (1768 - 1848) and is something of a tourist attraction even to those who haven't read his over-wrought novels. The Grand Bé is accessible only at low tide by a narrow causeway that has posted a warning about incoming tides all along its length: DO NOT ATTEMPT TO RETURN IF THE TIDE HAS RISEN OVER THE CAUSEWAY. IF YOU ARE CAUGHT BEHIND THE WATER, YOU MUST SPEND THE NIGHT ON THE ISLAND.

That *frisson* of danger -- *that's* why visitors flock to the Grand Bé.

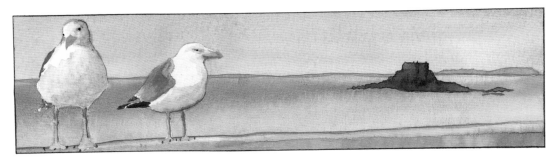

I am thrilled to see one of my favorite birds here -- the Herring Gull, called in French a *goéland argenté* (silvered gull). The air is filled with their raw cries -- *krah krah*, different from the sweet *cui cui* (cwee cwee) sound that little French song birds make. Ducks in France quack a harsh *coin coin* (qwaeh, qwaeh) sound -- this is important to know, in Saint-Malo, and here's why:
A great number of French Canadian tourists come to Saint-Malo, the birthplace of their founding father, **Jacques Cartier.** I enjoy hearing their speech, which is very different from standard French in that it is extremely nasal and staccato, often stressing the final, vowel-filled syllable of each word. But it is not to everyone's taste. A Malouin shopkeeper I spoke with groused that to him, listening to a **Quebécois** speak French is like listening to a **duck.** I had to laugh: it's funny because it's so **mean,** and so **true.**   I wonder what kind of bird I sound like when I speak French?

Chic

à la Coco Chanel

Femme Fatale

à la Brigitte Bardot

Gamine

à la Audrey Tautou

Bretons have always had sea water in their blood -- and the *Marinière* shirt on their backs. The stripes, they say, make it easier to find a sailor who's fallen into the drink -- it's a life-or-death race when there's a man overboard in the cold *Mor-Breizh*, between hypothermia and the *Mari Morgans* (Celtic mermaids) who lurk in these waters waiting for the chance to kidnap drowning men.

wool - 85€
cotton - 30€

Side trip to Cancale for the Complete Oyster Experience.

Ours is a mixed marriage: James loves oysters and I can't stand the sight of them. But this is James's honeymoon too, so there was no way that we were not going to spend a day in the oyster capital of France.

Mont St-Michel

Only nine miles from Saint-Malo, Cancale is a whole other climate. Its famous cove faces **east** and is protected from the wind and sea currents that hammer the rest of the Breton coast. Here, all is azure tranquillity, and oysters can rest peacefully in their vast beds, marinating in the plankton and the *joie du terroir* that makes them so **tasty**. Julius Caesar, Louis XIV, Napoleon, and now James Stone have gone to great lengths to get their Cancale oysters.

From the center of town it's a 4-mile hike down the cliffs, along the **Custom's Officer Walk** to the beach, where the *Ostréiculteurs* farm 25,000 tons of oysters a year. Rows of vendors all along the *quai* set out tents filled with trays of the day's harvest. The oysters are numbered 1 to 5 according to size and quality, No. 5 being the smallest; the *creuses* are the rare native oysters of France and the *plates* are the common Pacific oysters now raised here.

Unmistakably North Atlantic

is the connoisseur's verdict on the Cancale oyster. Also, they say, **Very briny with a hint of cucumbers.**

James buys a dozen *creuses* and sits with his plastic plate on the jetty, the low sea wall that separates us from the oyster beds.

Ever the diarist, I take notes:

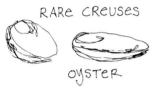

RARE CREUSES

OYSTER

J. says Cancale oysters taste: briny. salty. COLD.

He never ate them this close to their beds!
CHEW TWICE
(are oysters alive on the plate? They got a face? lungs? heart?)
Sloppy. Slurpy. Happy.

When he finishes, James just chucks the empty shells onto the beach as is the custom here. The beach is ankle-deep in oyster shells. All those oysters, billions of them, ripped from their husks, devoured as raw as Prometheus's liver.
Oh, the horror.

Scenes from Cancale:
Statue of
The Oyster Gatherers
of Cancale
near the church of
Saint-Méen
(yes, another Welsh
saint that nobody's ever
heard of).

How to take a 20-mile
bike ride in Brittany
with your three-month-
old golden retriever
puppy named Kimba.

Fun in French   *Huître* (meaning oyster) is one
of the most fun French words to say: *Wheat-ruh.* Cute.
I also love saying **hippopotamus** in French: *Eee-po-po-*
tame. All those wee syllables, like the sound of a tooth
fairy toe-dancing on your pillow...it certainly does *not*
sound like a 4,000-pound artiodactyl. And, when I tell
my husband that I need five more minutes to get ready,
I get a kick out of saying *Hold on, I need to* **ranger mes**
cheveux. **Arranging my hairs:** it just makes me laugh.
      Years ago I worked in New York with an
English woman, a terrible snob who was fond of large
silk shawls and velvet headbands. Once, when she was
giving her opinion in a staff meeting about a project we
were working on, she concluded her critique with the
words "*n'est-ce pas*?" It became a departmental in-joke,
which in turn became a running gag, to see who come up
with the most *soigné* French phrase in the heaviest
Cockney accent. Fun times.

The spirits of Saint-Malo.

The cobblestones come from the old Druid quarries from the interior of Brittany. The pavements are rumored to include slabs dug up from the ruins of the Roman Temple of Mars at **Corseul**. And from the Viking island **Chausey** come giant granite building blocks, same as the monks used to build Mont St-Michel a thousand years ago. Brownish-grey in daylight, the stones change color at dusk, become a brooding, breathing **Celtic Bleu**. It's as if they are sensate, mutable. Well, this is Brittany, after all, where everything in nature is **ensouled**.

Tip: **Always** book a three-day minimum stay at Saint-Malo as a precaution. The weather here can be ruinous when it comes to the main event: **the sunsets.** Heavy cloud cover from the stormy North Atlantic has a bad habit of moving in on this coast at twilight. On my honeymoon, I'm prepared to stay *a* **week** if that's what it takes, but we're in luck-- two nights in a row the air stays clear and even warm, and our twilight picnic on the ramparts gives us a capital-R **Romantic** view of the epic Emerald Coast.

Sunset in Saint-Malo

O God, Thy sea is so great, and my boat is so small.
Breton Fisherman's Prayer

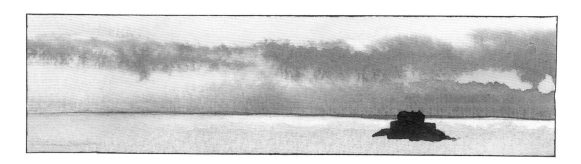

Voile

.Voile
.Pret-à-porter . Néoprène
.Ameublement . Cuir

Bayeux

Pontorson

Normandy & Brittany
sketchbook

Pierre
Tiercelin

☎ 60.24.53

montres
pendules

Pontorson

in St-Malo long after
sun set in a
bar that has
SWINGS.

The barman tells us that
he knows New York very
well, he goes there
every Christmas, on his
way to Rio de Janeiro
for New Year's eve.

Suddenly I feel a lot less
like the world traveler I
thought I was.

What I spend a lot of my →
travel time doing

les p'tits cats of Normandy
from the coat of arms of
William the Conqueror
2 cats = Norman flag
3 cats = English flag

Ermine on the coat of
arms of St-Malo.

Ermine in the flag
of Brittany.

The
FELINES & ERMINES
of FRANCE
No wonder I
love it here.

VILLA REMEMBER

This is me drawing this, on the outskirts of St-Malo

VILLA REMEMBER

108

Postcard from the Fork in the Road

FRANCE

Les mégalithes de Carnac 0,53€

The Romans called the woodland interior of Brittany simply The Wilderness. They'd seen the ruins, the great pillars of stone, the altars to alien gods — and they were frightened. Too much power in those ancient sacred places. They stayed away, left the forest to the barbarian Gauls & Franks, for their savage worship & secrets.

"Come on! It'll be fun!" I said, coaxing James to make a one-day detour on our way to Bordeaux. This is our chance to venture into the legendary Celtic Argoad , the holy primeval forest of interior Brittany, to see the standing stones they call The Alley of the Druids.

"It's just a quick little side trip -- what could go wrong? " I said.

And so we headed for the Forêt de Fougères.

Phase Five: The Going Gets Tough

Survival Tips.

The Going Gets Tough.

You know it's coming. We all know it -- the Honeymoon Phase doesn't last forever. Sooner or later, we all know that some real life shit is going to hit the fan. Suddenly Mr. Perfect drives you crazy, out of the blue Ms. Right is a huge pain in the butt. Most of us have the good sense to understand that that's just the way life is: it g tough sometimes. And most of us don't let a bad day or two ruin the whole love affair. Except for travelers. They **never** see it coming, and when the going gets tough they get all bent out of shape.

Travel, as we all know, is a heightened experience. That's why we love it so. But that intensity also has a down side. You know the saying, **Familiarity Breeds Contempt?** It was probably coined by traveling companio Heck: even **God** can get on your nerves on a long road trip.

Wandering with God through the Sinai Desert, His people often grew restless and rebellious of His ever-presence. Their annoyance grew in spite of His miraculous provisions of food and amusements along the way: sweet water and a lo-cal carbohydrate called *manna* (from Heaven, no less), pillars of fire and cloud. They even tried to ditch him altogether in favor of a golden calf. The whole trip must have worn on God's love, too, because once they all got where they were going He's never taken His people on that kind of journey again.

Christopher Columbus (captain of the Santa Maria) and **Martin Alonzo Pinzon** (the captain of the Pinta) were good friends when they set sail on the famous first voyage to the New World in 1492. But they began to get on each other's nerves as soon as they touched down in Hispaniola. Disagreements over their itinerary and their booty got so bad that on the return voyage to Spain Columbus threatened to *hang* Pinzon in the middle of the Atlantic Ocean. The stress of the voyage, and of having to defend himself from Columbus' malicious persecution even after they had returned to home port, led to Pinzon's early death (at age 52) in 1493.

Rather early on during their 1857-58 trek in Africa to discover the source of the Nile, the partnership of explorers **Richard Burton and John Speke** began to unravel. By the time they arrived at Lake Tanganyika they were bitter enemies. They headed back to England on separate caravans and spent the next six years viciously challenging the truthfulness of each other's published African memoires. It's widely speculated that the bad blood between Speke and Burton is the reason for Speke's death, in 1864, from a self-inflicted gunshot wound.

Johnny Rotten had always known that his childhood friend **Sid Vicious** was a nitwit, but it never really bothered him until they took a cross-country road trip of America together, touring with their band The Sex Pistols, in 1978. At the final stop in San Francisco, Johnny Rotten stood up on stage at the Winterland Ballroom in front of a sell-out crowd of 5,400 and raged, "This is no fun -- at all. No fun." He turned on his heels, walked out, and never saw Sid again. Sid killed himself the following year.

My friends (let's call them Bart and Muffy) were going to spend four months traveling in India. But after just three weeks on the road they had become sick of each other. They arrived in Jaipur barely on speaking terms. "India can be overwhelming, " Muffy says. "All I wanted, after three weeks, was air-conditioning and a mall." Good thing there are **seven** malls in Jaipur. "We picked the one with a Pizza Hut," she says.

They spent four days there, in the mall. "We went to movies, ate McDonald's French fries, got a much-needed dose of normalcy," Bart explains. They did not visit a single temple, bazaar, museum, garden, or monument in The Pink City (hence the pseudonyms). But they left Jaipur rejuvenated and back in sync with one another, and succeeded in finishing their journey without further incident. They are still married, and planning another long road trip for next year. For the moral of this story, see below.

Calamities are unavoidable, in love and travel.
All it takes to make it to the end of the road
are some good **Survival Tips.**

Survival tips for love and travel.

Keep at least two feet between you and the penguins in the South Pole. Penguins are known for their "horizontal projectile defecation" -- poop shoots out of them like rockets. It stinks, it stains, and it's very sticky; it is almost impossible to wash out of clothing or to scrape off boots.

If you should find it necessary to jump into icy water, make sure that you jump in naked. Wet clothes suck all your body heat right out of you, even after you have made your way to dry land. However, if you are fully clothed, roll around in the snow: it will act like a towel, absorbing water from your garments.

Just because you can't stand the sight of each other doesn't mean you aren't still in love. It just means you're having a bad day. **Relax.**

When glacier trekking, it helps to be greatly overweight. That is, **fat.** Skinny people fall into crevasses and slide so far down into those deep cracks that they are beyond the reach of rescuers.

Greenhorns on the cattle drive: until you're broken in, wear pantyhose under your jeans. This will provide you with an extra layer of insulation between you and your mount and prevent saddle sores.

Upon meeting bears in the wilderness, don't act like bear food. If you meet cannibals, don't act like lunch.

Allow each other to make three stupid mistakes per day. Count each stupidity-free day as a blessing.

The most likely way to die in a rain forest is to be hit by tree branches falling from the canopy (which can be as high as a 30-story building). Wear a helmet.

The leading cause of death in the Caribbean is a hit on the head by a coconut. Wear a helmet.

Each morning, look at yourself in the mirror and say: "You're no bargain either."

There are approximately 6,500 spoken languages in the world but **screaming** is universal.

In Africa, stay out of rivers and lakes. If you do swim, towel off immediately to rid yourself of the water-born schistosomiasis-infected grubs that will latch onto your skin and bore into your body. A minor itch afterwards means that you have not got them all; report to a field hospital immediately. Also, even if it is 105°, always wear long sleeves and trousers to avoid the bite of the black fly (river blindness) or the tsetse fly (sleeping sickness).

The hippopotamus is the deadliest animal in Africa. Even man-eating crocodiles run away from hippos, who can weigh up to 7,000 pounds. Plus, they have 20-inch teeth, bullets bounce off their skin, and they can out-run any human (hippos have been clocked doing 22 mph). Luckily, they only eat grass: camp on sandy, grassless areas to avoid them.

If caught outdoors in an open space during a thunder storm, minimize your contact with the ground by standing on your tippy-toes. If struck by lightning, a bolt will pass right through your body more quickly (less damage to internal organs) than if you're standing flat-footed.

If marooned on a desert island, dig a trench running north to south (you'll be exposed to a lesser amount of sunlight in that direction) and lie in it. For additional shade, pile up more sand on three sides.

If mugged by knife: Drop to the ground and curl up to protect your torso (**the kill zone**); kick at the attacker's knees or groin. If mugged by gun: Turn and run, screaming as loud as you can. The odds are only 50-50 that the gunman will try to shoot a moving target, and only 40-60 that he'll hit you if he tries.

Any problem in the world can be solved by dancing. So says James Brown, the Godfather of Soul. **So dance.**

Me with Stonehenge, 1976
(Hugging was prohibited in 1977 after public access to the site was restricted by the Historic Building and Monuments Commission for England.)

Me with Carnac, 1985
(Hugging was prohibited in 1991, after public access to the site was restricted by the Heritage Ministry of the French national government.)

A Crash Course on the Megaliths of Brittany

Megalithic sites can be found in Europe from Scandinavia to Sardinia. But the density and antiquity of such sites in Brittany suggest that the megalith-building culture began here, spreading north and east throughout the late Stone Age up until the Bronze Age (6000 BCE - 1200 BCE). No one knows who these megalith-builders were, where they came from, or why they disappeared.

The Breton language is used to describe megalithic monuments: *menhir* (long stone, for large upright standing stones); *dolmen* (table stone, for the large slab "cap" stone set across smaller supporting stones); and *cromlech* (curving rocks, used to describe circular constructions -- rare in Brittany -- such as Stonehenge).

Carnac, the pre-eminent megalithic site in Brittany (southern coast) is the oldest stone construction in Europe. With 3,000 individual *menhirs* in alignments dating from 4500 - 3300 BCE, it is older than the Pyramids of Egypt.

The megaliths were already ancient when the Celts moved into Brittany during the Iron Age, approx. 1000 BCE. The legend that the megalith-building culture was connected with the spiritual practices of the Celts was started in 1805 by the writer and civil servant Jacques Cambry (1749 - 1807), born in the town of Lorient 15 miles/24 km from Carnac. His book, *Celtic Monuments* proposed a romantic but unsubstantiated Breton/Celtic Druid stone culture responsible for the mysterious alignments and tombs found in his native Brittany and elsewhere. That same year he founded *l'Académie celtique*, the first antiquities preservation society in France.

The Alley of the Druids (*Le Cordon des Druides*) is an especially appealing site. It is exceedingly rare to find megaliths preserved deep in the woods, and the beech and chestnut groves of the *Forêt de Fougères* are so beautiful that they are believed to be part of the legendary "lost" druidical forest of Scissy.

I am **dying** to get to the forest of Fougères! The grandeur, solemnity, and situational **awesomeness** of **The Alley of the Druids** must be a cross between Stonehenge and Carnac!

I had it all planned.
That was my first mistake.

It sounded so perfect. A day in the woods -- not just any woods, but the old growth forest of the mystical *Forêt de Fougères*. A chance to wander among ancient Celtic standing stones -- not just any standing stones, but the standing stones called **The Alley of the Druids**. And at the end of the day, a stroll back into town -- not just any town but *Fougères*, a town so charming that it was beloved by Victor Hugo, Chateaubriand, and Balzac.

I study the maps, I research the transportation options, I scrutinize the timetables. The Fougères train station has been shut down so the bus was our only choice; two a day, 2 hours and 15 minutes for the 44-mile journey from Saint-Malo. We'd get off the bus at noon at **Place Aristide Briand**, at the Tourist Office -- which happens to be just across the street from one of the best hotels in town. We'd pick up tourist info about the forest, check into the hotel, head out to see us some awesome standing stones, be back in town in time for a leisurely cocktail hour before a romantic dinner, sleep, then continue on to an easy half-day journey to Bordeaux. Talk about efficient. **Champion A-Number-One Travel Planner**, *c'est moi*.

When we get to the Fougères Tourist Office there is some unforeseen good news! The girl handing us the map to *le forêt* tells us that *"C'est pas loin*, a city bus will take you there -- it's just on the edge of town."

I believed her. That was my second mistake.

Next, we cross the road to the Hôtel les Voyageurs. We don't have a reservation but that's not the problem. The problem is that the reception won't open until 2:30. For **crying out loud**, don't these people know that I have **a schedule??** And that schedule **does not** call for us to be hanging around an empty hotel lobby for two hours!!

I march off to find a phone booth to call other hotels, but my damn phone card doesn't work no matter how hard I pound the damn thing into the damn thingy. I stomp back to James, cursing the French tourism and telecom industries. James sees me coming and strolls in the opposite direction. This makes me livid. I **hate** it that he's so calm **when I have a schedule!!** I decide to teach him a lesson. I, too, will go in the opposite direction. See how he likes them apples.

I storm out onto the street, pound my way down tiny cobblestone *rues* to the moats of the town's famous 12th-century *château*. I am mad as hell the whole way, virtuous and angry and blowing off a lot of steam. I'm not sure what lesson I'm teaching James by abandoning him in the middle of Fougères but it's a **good** one yessiree. I spitefully browse the souvenir shops, buy some post cards, forgo the tour of the castle, follow some tourists along a path that leads to the beautiful and restful public gardens. That's where I run into James, coming my way.

"I was looking for you everywhere!" he exclaims, as I act maddeningly unconcerned, as part of my plan to teach him a lesson. "It's a small town," I shrug; "I figured we'd meet up sooner or later."

"I was checking us into the hotel and you disappeared!" he says. It seems that while I was trying to make my phone calls back at the hotel, J. had roused the manager -- I'd missed his signal to follow him to the front desk. Well *pardonnez-moi*. Would it have killed him to have *said something?* I check my watch.

"We better hurry if we want to catch the 1:43 bus to the forest," I say.

We set off at a trot to the bus stop. It's hot, and it's uphill, but we make it in time. Finally, things are going our way. The bus driver is very nice to us dumb tourists *cherchez la forêt* and when he pulls up at what looks to be a derelict housing project at the end of his route, he tells us that this is where we get off. I look around. I see dingy concrete multi-level apartment blocks with laundry hanging out the windows. "*Où est la forêt?*" I ask.

"*Juste là*," the driver says, pointing to a line of trees in the distance. Oh. **The edge of town.** Not an **edge**, really, no, not edge-y at all; more like a vague woodsiness, creeping up a big hill, miles away from where I thought it would be. Oh well. A minor setback.

We trudge up the D177 to the woody fringe of the *Forêt de Fougères.* And then we walk on, and on, and on. Later I find out that the actual distance from the town of Fougères to the Alley of the Druids is six miles (10 km), if you don't get lost. Which we somehow manage to do.

From the entrance into the forest we head off on what we think is a picturesquely overgrown foot trail. For the first hour, as we crash through the thickets of primordial greenery (**fougères** means **ferns**, and there's a thousand years' worth of them here, and lots of forest too), I'm telling James, "This is so fantastic! The **way they've left the Alley of the Druids in situ in such an inaccessible and authentic location! So deep in the wild woods!!"**

And then it dawns on us that we're not getting any closer to the secret location of the most romantic standing stones in Brittany. In fact, we have no idea where we are. It's hot, and we are tired and hungry (having skipped lunch to hurry on to this journey) and we have to start all over.

Thanks to James' excellent sense of direction it only takes us an hour to get ourselves back where we started. Looking around carefully, we perceive a neatly cleared gravel lane. Following it for a quarter of a mile, we see a huge wooden sign on the shoulder, pointing right to it. The Alley of the Druids. I start to laugh. It's a *driveway*, for God's sake. As wide as a two-lane highway. We could have taken a **taxi**, had ourselves driven directly into the mythical heart of this mystical forest! Been here in 15 minutes!

And look at these so-called *megaliths!* They say there's **23 large standing stones** here, but most of them are only about three feet high. And they're strewn in a wayward zig-zag manner that takes real imagination to conjure an *alignment.* Standing stones? It all looks more like a bunch of random **laying-down-on-the-ground stones.**

The tallest stone, the grand-sounding **terminal menhir**, is only six feet (1.8 meters) tall. I don't even bother to hug it.

While we are collapsed on one of the nearby park benches (Yes! Park benches! And picnic tables!!), gathering up our strength for the hike back to the bus stop at the scary housing project six miles away, a car pulls up. Two Germans pop out. They have a dog with them -- his name is Easy -- and they happened to be passing by and thought they'd have a quick look at the famous *Forêt de Fougères.* I eye their water bottles but parched as I am, I'm too polite to ask. They don't seem all that friendly anyway: "We can't give you a lift into town," one of them says, reading the desperate look in my eyes; "Our back seat is full of camping gear." They hop in their VW and diesel down the road.

James and I haul ourselves back to the D177 for the long march. But wait. I see a sign for something on the other side of the road, in the other side of the forest: *La Pierre du Trésor.* The Treasure Stone, another prehistoric Celtic megalith, and it's only 1/3 of a mile (800 meters) away. "Oh come on come on come on," I whine; "We're never coming back to the Fougères Forest ever again in our whole lives -- let's at least see The Treasure Stone as long as we're here!!" That was my last mistake.

I head back into the woods, James reluctantly following me, down a long narrow trail that ends in a small clearing. I stop and scan the landscape. There's not a *pierre* in sight. And then I look down.

The Treasure Stone is a jumble of five moldy slabs of rock lying on the ground. I only know this because of the wooden sign, in the form of an arrow, pointing at them, on which is written *La Pierre du Trésor.* I can't *wait* to tell J., who is just now coming into the clearing, but I'm laughing too hard to get the words out, doubled over and staggering in circles, just too delighted with the way this whole day has turned out, laughing and laughing and laughing.

James stares at the rock pile without expression. He looks at me. These are the last words he will speak to me for the next four hours: *"You gotta be fucking kidding me."*

He doesn't say another thing the whole time we are tramping back into town on the D177, sticking our thumbs out at motorists blasting past us at 100kph. He is silent the whole time we languish in the busted-up bus shelter at the housing project, waiting for the day's last city bus to roll into view. He says nothing as we board the 18:00h to Fougères *(ville)* and slump exhaustedly in our seats, trying not to act as unwashed, unlucky, and undone as we feel. He's still mum as we get off and drag ourselves into the *supermarché* near our hotel, grab several liter-bottles of Evian, and stand by until the cashier is finished throwing out some shoplifting drug addicts so we can pay for the first drink of water we've had since breakfast. Well, to tell the truth, I wasn't much in the mood for *badinage* anyway.

Le Forêt de Fougères

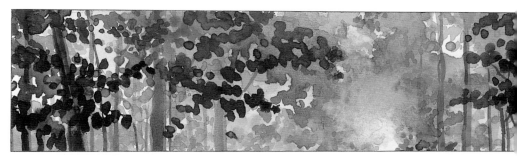

The Fougères Forest

Le Cordon des Druides
The Alley of the Druids

La Pierre du Trésor
The Treasure Stone

It is only after we've showered and James is pouring us each a slug of well-earned wine that we trust ourselves to speak. He raises his glass and toasts: "Well, let's hope that this is as bad as it gets," he says, and smiles. "Oh, it is, it is," I say, as if this is a once-in-a-road-trip kind of day.

We are too tired, sore, and dispirited to do much for dinner except choose the nearest available restaurant for limp, luke-warm Italian food served by an absent-minded waitress in a dirty uniform with drug addict friends in the bar (there do seem to be an awful lot of skinny, grimy, homeless-looking youths in Fougères). We're sure this is the worst meal to be had in France. We were sure, that is, until we get to Bordeaux the next night and are having what is **truly** the most dismal on-the-road-dining experience possible.

It started out well. We had a fine breakfast at a café where the *propriétaire* made a fuss to get me his finest tea (an Assam that he kept in a special jar behind the bar). So we cleared out of town with no hard feeling towards Fougères. Refreshed, relaxed, and once again eager for adventure, we got on the bus to the Rennes train station.

Suffice it to say that the five-hour trip from Rennes to Bordeaux took twice that long, thanks to a disabled train in Nantes, a long detour to Tours, garbled track announcements and a missed connection to Poitiers, and a last-minute dive onto a TGV for which we had no tickets. This is how we arrive at 9 o'clock in the evening in Bordeaux in the middle of a sold-out city-wide event (it's either a marathon or a film festival; we are too tired and too uninterested to find out for sure) so that we end up in the only vacancy we can find, at midnight, a stuffy attic room in a last-resort hotel on Bordeaux's noisiest street with no viable options for dinner except what's in James' pockets: a chocolate bar and half a bottle of Evian.

Every road trip needs a low point.

This truth comes to me as I lie sleepless in that dingy, sweltering attic room. This is not my first road trip, and it's not my first marriage either. I know that my hissy fit in Fougères and our bad luck on the road to Bordeaux does not spell doom for either our love affair or our journey. Love affairs are like road trips, and road trips are like love affairs -- from beginning to end the emotions are equally intense, the phases just as predictable. Love and travel. They both have their ups and downs.

   This is the thought that keeps me company until dawn, when I finally fall asleep.

Phase Six: In The Comfort Zone.

Ready for the long haul.

In The Comfort Zone.
Real love, real travel, ready for the long haul.

If **road trips** are like **love affairs**, both following the same predictable course of ups and downs (which is the whole point of this book), then the **Comfort Zone** is where we all want to end up. Having toughed it out, worked our way through the bad days, making it past the problems and troubles that were thrown in our way, we can now take **pride** in getting **this far**, to a place where we feel happy, safe, and successful. We've made it! We're survivors! We could do this forever! And it feels *great*.

Yes, here in the **Comfort Zone** is where we feel we **belong**, where we feel as if this journey we're on has become our second nature. And here is where we are tempted to turn all these good feelings into a commitment to a more permanent and lasting way of life.

When we are in love, this is where we turn our **affair** into a **relationship**.

When we are on the road, this is where we turn into **vagabonds**.

How To Vagabond
Tips from the Great Hobos of the Past

Matsuo Basho
Basho (1644 - 1694) was already a poet of some renown in Japan when he gave up his teaching post in Edo **at age 40** to become a vagabond. Of his many journeys, his most famous is the 150-day/1,200-mile walk he took along the north and east coasts of Honshu. It was on this journey that he kept a travel diary, a mix of prose and verse, which he later published as *Narrow Road to a Far Province*, in which he invented a new kind of poetry -- the **haiku**.

- Travel Light. All you need for a season's journey is a cotton robe, a lunch box, a rain coat, calligraphy supplies, sandal-buying money, a hat, and extra stockings to keep you warm on cold nights.
- Also, bring a journal. Write in it nightly.
- Be less introspective, more attuned to nature.
- Record everything -- the sleepless nights, the fleas in the mattress, the kindnesses shown to you by strangers on the road, the conversation of bores.

Count Leopold Berchtold
The Count (1759 - 1809), a Czech nobleman by birth, spent **seventeen years** vagabonding throughout Europe and the Turkish Empire, publishing widely read tracts on the philosophy of travel. This is from his most famous one, the *Essay to Direct and Extend the Inquiries of Patriotic Travelers (1789)*:

- In dealing with the lower classes, one must disguise one's rank in order to encourage communication.
- The three skills most necessary for the successful socialization with local inhabitants of foreign lands are swimming, drawing, and playing a portable instrument such as a flute.
- Peasants who live in remote provinces, rather than in cities, are best subjects for one's inquiries. They are wiser in folk ways, and one's inquiries will attract less suspicion.
- Seek local persons of reputed genius and eccentricity, interview them for ideas and advice that will be of value to humankind. Take notes quickly and furtively, lest one be conspicuous or taken as a spy.

Servas International, founded in 1949 in Norway, is a world-wide network of travelers whose purpose is to build peace and goodwill through positive interactions during international journeys. Here are their Top Three rules:

- Learn in advance about the places you are going to, but do not think you ever know more than the people who live there.
- Be aware of others' reactions to your behavior in order to judge what is acceptable. Respect their differences and their right to behave as they choose. If you think a person is behaving offensively, remember that good manners aren't necessarily the same in all countries. Perhaps they think you are behaving offensively too.
- **Do not** criticize other people's countries, not even about the **weather** or the **conditions of the roads.** In most cases, there is nothing anyone can do about them, and it only makes the locals feel defensive.

John Steinbeck (1902 - 1968), winner of the Nobel Prize for Literature, wrote *Travels With Charley* (1960) about his 10,000-mile journey across America, from Maine to California and back.

- A journey must have a design -- everything in the world must have a design or the human mind rejects it. (Steinbeck drove from his home on Long Island to properly **begin** his journey in **Maine,** for design reasons.)
- One must be **vacilando** when one travels. **Vacilando,** from the Spanish verb **vacillar.,** has nothing to do with vacillating. If one is **vacilando,** he is going somewhere but doesn't greatly care whether he gets there or not. For example, say you want to be **vacilando** in the streets of Mexico City. Choose some object that is almost certain not to exist there, and then diligently try to find it. (Steinbeck went to Maine to see potatoes, but really didn't mind whether he saw potatoes or not. He ended up seeing a lot of potatoes.)

James and I are ready to vagabond.   We've made it at last to Bordeaux, the ancient duchy of Aquitaine, and its stupendous wine country -- the most prestigious vineyards in the world. This is all **terra incognita** -- neither of us has ever been here before. So for the first time in France, we feel that we are in a truly foreign country -- here we are, with no pre-conceptions, totally open to new insights, ready for anything. And, **most important**, we are at ease with the road and each other. We are in the Comfort Zone.

So with the confidence of seasoned travelers, with no itinerary, timetable, or any previous experience of the place, we set out to discover ourselves and Bordeaux in **a vagabond frame of mind.**

It's as if we are starting out on a whole new trip, with a map full of blank space, a guide book full of blank pages. We feel like the venerable **Basho**, setting out to invent for ourselves a whole new travel **language.**

And so, without further ado, I present to you:

Vagabonding in Bordeaux, A to Z.

Acquired Taste.

Vagabonding is an acquired taste. And as in all acquired tastes (for bleu cheese, oysters, Calvados) a true *gourmet* knows just the right amount it takes to produce a peak experience. So as gourmet **travelers** we know that it's going to take at least four days to achieve a peak experience in the St-Emilion area vineyards. This stone farmhouse is our four-day *home address* in the Côtes de Castillon.

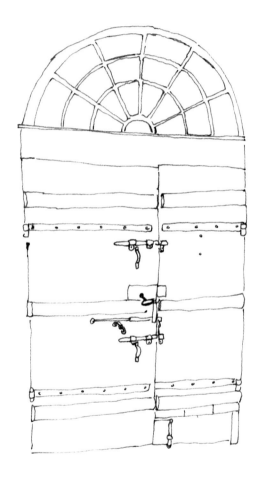

Actual size of the key to the front door.
And it was *heavy*, too.

I said to J., "This place would be perfect if it came with a cat."

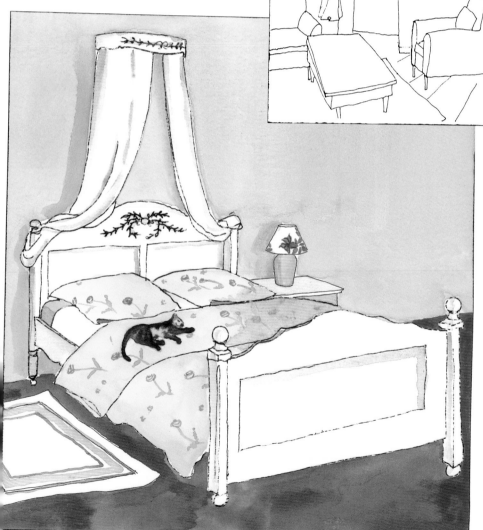

Meet **Amande**, our cat-away-from-home.

Beaten Tracks, On and Off Of.

The vineyards of Bordeaux are hardly on the outer edges of **civilization**. They are more like its crossroads: the Celts, Romans, Visogoths, and Franks all knew this land well; wine making has been going on here for over two thousand years. And then came the **Plantagenets**, a boisterous and large cast of characters that includes Richard the Lionhearted, Henry V, and the legendary **Eleanor of Aquitaine** -- there is a lot of history to see here besides what's on the vine. And that's a good thing, too, because in spite of Bordeaux being the world's most beloved wine, getting a good, do-it-yourself up-close look at the stuff on its home turf is **almost impossible**.

The wine makers of Bordeaux are renowned for being aristocratic, old-fashioned, and snobbish. They have not welcomed wine tourists the way Napa Valley in California has. So what if the Californians make a billion dollars a year off their visitors? *Quelle horreur*! The *viti-culteurs bordelaise* sniff in distaste at the idea that their *châteaux* should be open to just **anyone**. So, of the 8,000 estates producing wine in Bordeaux, only half a dozen offer tours, on a very limited schedule, at prices designed to appeal to only the "luxury tourist."

　　　Maybe because of this grudging attitude towards visitors, very few foreigners venture into this corner of France. Statistics from the **Comité Régional du tourisme d'Aquitaine** (for 2002 and 2004) tell the story: 80% of the visitors to Bordeaux *are French people from other parts of France*. And of the tiny cohort of foreign visitors here, 85% come from Europe. Minus from that the rich Russians, Chinese, and South Americans who come here to stock up their private cellars, and vagabonds like James and me are on our **own** here, bushwhacking the back roads from **Libourne** to **Lussac**. And that's fine with us.

Cruise Control.

As travelers, J. and I are dawdlers, and not particularly dedicated to sight-seeing or shopping. But we are eager to **carpe diem** this leg of the road trip.

So we rent a car.

FESTINA LENTE,

Erasmus used to say:

HASTEN SLOWLY.

That's our plan exactly.

See as much of life as possible, but take time to **notice** it too.

Desiderius Erasmus of Rotterdam (1466 - 1536) was the greatest wandering philosopher of the Renaissance. His work became part of the founding tenets of the Age of Enlightenment.

So he should know.

The entire village of St-Philippe d'Aiguilhe, a few miles north-east of St-Emilion.

Dharma Bums go by many names. Old Travelers is what Mark Twain called them in his day, those millionaires on the Grand Tour. Lately, I've heard them called Travel Nazis -- identified by their dreadlocks, tribal tattoos, and general scruffiness. In any case, beware the Dharma Bums. They are the self-appointed experts on the Truth of Travel. They have already been everywhere, seen everything, become enlightened twice before breakfast, and done it for less money, in half the time, and with more authenticity than *you* ever could.

What they have in common, Mark Twain warns, is a "supernatural ability to bore". Us vagabonds have to resist the urge to turn into Dharma Bums, and to never forget the Number One Rule of the Road: Travel never made anyone interesting. See next page.

Epiphanies.

Go easy. There is nothing inherently edifying about travel. The universe seldom reveals itself in grand visions except to prophets and saints, which probably leaves you out no matter how far from home you roam. In everyday life, on and off the road, it's the little things that count, the small awarenesses that illuminate your place on the Wheel of Life. Beware any idea bigger than a breadbox.

Shortly before I left home to go on a two-year mission in the Sahara I sought out an old Africa hand for advice. He'd been administering land management projects in the desert for 20 years, under dictators and during revolutions, through drought and famine and the occasional flood. I spoke to him, hoping he wouldn't notice the panic in my voice: "What's the most important thing I need to know about living in Africa?" I asked.

He looked thoughtful, took a sip of beer, set the bottle back carefully on the tabletop. "Always walk in the shade," he said.

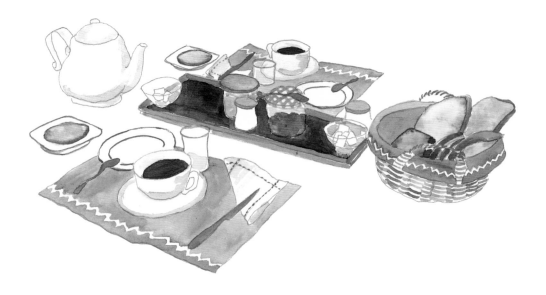

Breakfast served in the *salle à manger.*

Dinner self-catered, dished up in our *chambre.*

Feasting,

Guzzling, and

Haute Digestion.

Lunch in Bordeaux.

The soul of the day.

Lunch is a spiritual activity in France. All morning long, French workers put up with the insult to their *liberté* and *fraternité* that comes from having a *job*. So at lunchtime they take a two-to-four hour break in the day as a form of mutiny. Office workers, traffic wardens, college professors, shop girls, car mechanics, accountants -- up and down the social scale, French workers do not have our Puritan need to mortify the flesh. No one in France feels redeemed by workaholism. *Au contraire.* They feel instead a need to redress the imbalance that work imposes on life, and they do that over a leisurely lunch when they *recherchent* the finer things in life. Good food, good drink, good conversation.

And when we're in France, we make like the French do.

The days are warmer than usual. Rains are light and rare -- the long lulling hours of sunshine fade gently into mild nights. Summer of 2005 has all the hallmarks of an extraordinary vintage year for Bordeaux. For wine and, especially, for lunch.

Feasting on *les spécialités bordelaises* means:

Gigot -- loin of milk-fed lamb
Grenier médocain -- pig stomach, charcuterie-style
Bécasse -- woodcock
Cèpes frais persillade -- mushroom stew

Huîtres Gravette -- local species of oysters
Lamproie -- locally fished eel
Alose -- locally fished shad
Esturgeon - local species of sturgeon

James can eat almost anything but I have the **gustatory equivalent of tone deafness**. Also, I am repulsed by food that looks grey and slithery (see: eel, pig stomach, oysters, and mushrooms, above). Good thing the French don't mind serving eggs for lunch -- I can always order an omelet.

But lunch in Bordeaux is not just about the food. It's about the quest to find that exquisite little out-of-the-way place where a kindly *madame* whips up her secret family recipes while a doting *monsieur* fusses with the guests, making sure that no one is ever saddened by an empty wine glass.

For us, it's not all that hard to detect the place that will be our perfect *restauration* experience for the day. We take it step-by-step:

Step One: We start looking early. The French take *le déjeuner* seriously and they are *à table* no later than 12:15. If we dawdle, we risk losing out on the *plat du jour* that everyone else has lined up for, and have to settle for the more expensive *menu gastronomique*. A *gastronomique* menu is code for *piège à touriste* (tourist trap).

Step Two: We check the menu for signs of age. The menu, which by law must be displayed outside the premises, should be freshly hand-lettered. Faded ink tells us that the menu has not been changed lately, a sign that the chef isn't shopping around for in-season *spécialités*.

Step Three: We check the parking lots. The locals know where to find the best food. So we look for cars with local registrations in the parking lot (it's all on the license plate: the car's reg. no. begins with the *département* no. -- so in Bordeaux we're looking for cars from Gironde 33, Dordogne 24, and Lot-et-Garonne 47). If the restaurant is good enough for the locals, it's good enough for us.

Step Four: We look for the cat. The best places lack *décor* in the formal sense, yet still have a peppy *je ne sais quoi* sense of themselves -- framed family portraits on the wall, vintage net curtains on the door, a resident calico cat passing judgment on the clientele. The cat is crucial.

Step Five: Having determined that the place meets all our criteria, we settle in and wait for enlightenment.

The **Haut-Médoc** is a narrow thirty-mile long strip on the bank of the Gironde estuary directly north of the city of Bordeaux. To the west the vineyards are protected from the salty winds of the Atlantic Ocean by pine forests; to the east the morning sun gives them long, warm days with soft transition to gentle night. The red wines of the Haut-Médoc are, quite simply, the best in the world. As wine expert H. Warner Allen once described them, they are **an heroic drink as might refresh the warring archangels.**

Dégustez nos VINS d' origine

Guzzling in Bordeaux.

Connoisseurship in wine, they say, requires a **profound amount of self-knowledge.** I don't know if that's unique to wine. I find that it takes a penetrating self-awareness to buy myself shoes, choose a hair style, pick a color to paint my kitchen.

But what the heck. I'm willing to peer deeply into my wine-self every day at lunch, see what's there. After all, we *are* in **wine country.** And isn't this why we travel? To *learn* about ourselves?

The geography and classifications of Bordeaux wine are complex. It is the largest wine-growing district on Earth: there are 284,000 acres (460 square miles) of vineyards here near the mouth of the Aquitaine basin where the Dordogne and Garonne rivers meet to form the Gironde estuary. The region is further divided into 19 sub-regions, containing 8,000 vineyards producing six generic and 60 prestigious *appellations d'origine contrôlée* (AOCs).

In other words, the place is lousy with *terroir*, that mystical combination of soil, itty-bitty micro-climate, and cultivation that gives a distinct character and spirit to each individual wine. So my first step to wine self-awareness is to focus my drinking on the *terroirs* that brought me here in the first place: the aristocratic gravel-strewn flatlands of the Haut-Médoc., and the picturesque clay slopes of the St-Emilion region.

St-Emilion is the wine that James collects. There are a thousand vineyards covering the pretty misty hills of this region, producing a wine that is often called "elegant"; rich and fruity but not "big", like the mighty California reds -- St-Emilions are more like swan-divers than weight-lifters. The neighboring communes of Pomerol and Côtes de Castillion produce similarly excellent wines.

The Official Wine Glass of the
Institut National des Appellations d'Origine

Height: 6" (27 cm)
Capacity: 7 ¾ oz. (US) (23 cl)
Origin: French technocrats
Cost: approx. $4.00 each

Notes: The form was standardized in 1970 -- its wide base and short stem gives this vessel a user-friendly heft and stability. It is a *tasting* glass, designed to heighten a beverage's characteristics both good and bad, and is said to favor the complexities of Bordeaux wines while murdering Burgundies.

The Riedel Sommeliers' Bordeaux Grand Cru

Height: 10 ½" (27 cm)
Capacity: 30 oz. (US) (90 cl)
Origin: Family of expert glassmakers from Austria
Cost: $100 each (hand-made of mouth blown lead crystal)

Notes: Since its design in 1959 this glass has been the connoisseurs' choice. Painstakingly crafted by master artisans, the generous bowl gives breathing space to both young and mature wines and the tulip form showcases the texture and bouquet of the world's most inscrutable beverage. To its fans, this glass offers an incomparable drinking experience that reveals the full majesty and intensity of the great Bordeaux wines that start at $1,000 a bottle.

The Official At-Home Wine Glass of James Stone

Height: 4" (10 cm)
Capacity: 8 oz. (US) (24 cl)
Origin: Kitchen cupboard, the one above the sink
Cost: $3.49 each, includes 13 oz. (370 g.) of jam

Notes: Yes, my husband will drink a Grand Cru from a jam jar, but not just **any** jam jar. It has to be *this* jam jar, which comes with his favorite raspberry preserves made by **Bonne Maman** (imported from France).

Haute Digestion.

Isabella Bird Bishop (1831 - 1904) bravely roamed the world on her own, writing popular books about her travels to the hinterlands of Australia, Asia, the Himalayas, the Pacific Islands, the Rockies. When asked what it was that made this prim Englishwoman so very valiant in foreign lands, her husband answered that the lady had **"the digestion of an ostrich."**

Ostriches, by the way, have since antiquity been reputed to be able to eat iron ore without sickening. And it's exactly that kind of guts that a vagabond needs. I'll say it: Travelers are bedeviled by a lot of disgusting foreign food on this planet. Here's a brief survey of the kinds of things the world traveler has to contend with:

Grilled sea horse
Barbeque scorpions
Roast silk worm
Skinned roast bat
Fried baby wasps
Sour ram's testicles
Rotten shark
Rotten loon

Blubber-wrapped
 seal flipper
Monkey
Chewy parrot
Caribou tongue
Mite Cheese
Jellied moose nose

Here in south-west France the foods I most want to avoid are *foie gras* (the liver of force-fed geese) and *pibales* -- little baby eels that wriggle like miniature cobras when they are boiled alive. And though the locals brag that their snails, the *Petit Gris* that are specially fed on barley, are ten times more mouthwatering than the more famous *escargots de Bourgogne*, I am not tempted.

I hope my vagabonding privileges won't be revoked just because I've become indifferent to exotic foods in my middle age.

Wine-drinking at lunch tends to make for sketchy food notes. But I would feel unworthy if I could not comment (even vaguely) on the grand cuisine of the **Aquitaine**.

In Ste-Foy-la-Grande I had an omelet with some marvelous kinds of exotic savory herbs, and in St-Emilion James had "tuna infused with V---------", which I can't remember now what the V stands for. There was James's "gratin de fishy stuff" in Pauillac and in Libourne I note that his *rouget* was delicious. I was always pleased with the *haricots verts*, and J. assures me that the *moules* and other *délices de l'Estuaire de la Gironde* were excellent.

Next page:
Top: To eat salad in France: **fold**, do not **cut**, the leaves.

Middle: Grilled black bass with lettuce-butter sauce; Three goat cheese medallions served on *pain grillé* drizzled with *herbes aromatiques*.

Bottom: *Moules marinières*; Chicken in a creamy garlic sauce with peppers on a bed of watercress.

Isn't it Ironic?

France is the world's **Number One** tourist destination -- **75 million** international travelers will journey here this year. This is *twice the* number of people who will journey to the world's no. 2 tourist destination (a tie between Spain and the USA, at around 35 million each). And the irony is that the French are the **least-traveled** people in the world: 85% of French people take their vacations in-country.

They just don't like to leave home: data compiled by the U.S. census bureau tabulates that only 740,000 *Français* have immigrated to America since 1820, a number that is *miniscule* compared to the *tens of millions* of Europeans who fled the continent during the same time period to escape war, revolution, famine, and poverty. Nope: nothing budges the French from their *beau pays.* No matter what, the French **stay put.**

Now, there might be unique and profound social and cultural reasons why the French don't get a move on. But in view of the fact that for the rest of humanity a trip to France is the *nec plus ultra* of the **romance** and **prestige** of world travel, the natives' stick-in-the-mud-ness strikes me as really sweet.

Only the French could get away with being so provincial.

A 18h30
Soirée Country
apéritif gratuits
REPAS MEXICAIN
18 €

The sign in the café made me curious. A Soirée Country? With Mexican food? In Bordeaux? *In St-Philippe d'Aiguille?* This I have to see.

It looks as if every one of the town's 431 inhabitants, every man, woman, and child, has come out to the enormous tent erected in a clearing in the vineyards. But *where* could they have got all those cowboy hats?

It is nothing if not a love-in for the American West. Every single person here is in cowpoke mode-- jeans, fringed jackets, cowboy boots, yoked shirts. On stage the band, brought in specially from Quebec, belts out country and western hits and the dance floor is full of gingham-dressed gals doing the latest line dance out of Laredo. The music is loud and the crowd favorite is a Carl Perkins song called *Mile Out of Memphis* -- that one they have to do twice in a row.

"I'll be right back," James says to me, and he jogs down the road to our rented farmhouse. He returns ten minutes later wearing his Grateful Dead T-shirt. Well, tie-dye is as close to country as we Long-Islanders can get.

We sit at a long table full of French cowboys drinking red wine. I ask one ranch hand decked out in a black leather Harley-Davidson vest if he's ever been to America; he takes a long, existential drag on his Marlboro: "*C'est mon rêve,*" he says.

We leave at midnight and when we wake the next morning, a little hung over, we can hear the country music in the distance, the party still going strong.

J is for Jaded.

Sometimes it feels as if **everybody** has already been **everywhere**. Average Americans take family vacations in Bali. English yobbos flock to Sri Lanka for their holidays. The Chinese Communists take shopping trips to Paris, teenagers sail solo around the world, and twelve-year olds are racing each other to be the youngest person to summit Mount Everest.

Don't let this make you **jaded**. Because we are a nosey, restless, wandering species and **travel** is what we **do**. And there is **no time** like the **present** to see for yourself this marvelous, strange, lonely and lovely little blue tourist attraction called Earth. And years from now, when you look around at the hordes that crowd the souvenir stands in every jungle and desert of this beloved and abused planet, you will look back on your journeys and you will be happy that you went when the **going was good**.

And besides, there are still undiscovered places like **La Réole**, which we had all to our tourist-selves on a fine September day. La Réole (pop. 4,000) is reached by driving over the Garonne River on a suspension bridge that was designed by **Gustave Eiffel**. It boasts of having the oldest town hall in all of France, built for **Richard the Lionhearted** in 1171 when he was the newly anointed Duke of Aquitaine.

On one of La Réole's historic cobblestone streets I am lost in time as I watch a young man approach a small box mounted on an ancient stone wall. He fiddles with it, pulls a small packet out of it, and hurries away. I realize that it's the town's lone vending machine and I mosey over to examine this unique cultural artifact.

The machine sells condoms. I am *shocked*. I had half-expected mini-madrigals, or chain mail key chains, or mead-flavored chewing gum -- nothing so totally anachronistic as **condoms**, *right out on the street*. And then I'm shocked again, at how easily I am shocked ...there goes my claim to world-traveler blasé.

K is for the **K**arma of the Road.

"Il faut visiter Rauzan!" the hitchhiker says.

We've been searching for hitchhikers on these back roads of Bordeaux, a sense of obligation we have from all the times that we've been helped by strangers when we were thumbing rides in the 1970s and '80s. This young guy standing by the road out of St-Emilion is the first fellow vagabond that we've seen. It's 9 AM and he's drunk.

I've been walking since three o'clock this morning, he tells us after he's thanked us for stopping for him. *French people don't like hitch hikers,* he says. *I'm from Perpignan but I come every year to Bordeaux for the vendange. Are you going towards Rauzan?* he asks. We've never heard of the place. And it isn't in our guide book.

So we go to **Rauzan** (pop. 978). There isn't much to see here, just a *donjon* in a ruined castle that dates from the 13th - 15th century. I am on the verge of being bored when I **see** it: The Door.

They are life-sized, this merman and mermaid. And I get it: Rauzan is in the heart of the land known as *Entre Deux Mers --* Between Two Seas. Before there was wine here, there was water. The Romans called the land **Aquitania** (from **aqua,** Latin for **water**) for its **Atlantic Ocean** coastline to the west, the **Gironde** estuary to the north, and the two rivers that saturate its interior (archaically known as "inland seas"), the **Garonne** and the **Dordogne.**

The twin-tailed merfolk here come from the oldest stories of the Romans, who adopted this bit of mythology from the ancient Syrian cult of Atargatis, the mermaid goddess.

Oh, how I want this door. Oh, how I want to live in a place where people have the **birthright** to this door!

The
Low-Down on
Motorized
Nomading

Because both our cars at home have automatic transmissions I have never noticed how especially handsome my husband looks when he drives a stickshift -- that's the good thing about all the time we're spending in our rental car. Mile after mile, I have the opportunity to study James' driving in detail. Mile after mile, hour after hour. I have become *very* astute about his driving.

James and I met at a party. Small talking, he said that I didn't look old enough to remember the Monkees. "I'm 47," I told him. James had just turned 50; milestone birthdays fascinate me so I asked what he did to celebrate. "Nothing yet," he said "Not until I take a road trip in Bordeaux."

In our third month of dating we took our first road trip. We drove to J's favorite beach on the Long Island Sound, in Rhode Island. It was late in the day, perfect timing for a romantic dinner but bad for parking. At the last lot in town there's a guy holding up a scribbled sign on a skanky piece of cardboard: FULL. James said, "Do you think he makes a new sign every day?" I laughed so hard, I knew I had to marry him.

Our longest pre-France road trip was a five-day, 1,000-mile trip from Florida to Long Island, one week after James proposed. The hours that we spent in the car traveling on some pretty dull interstate highways were filled with a lively debate on the **One Hundred Greatest Songs of Our Lifetime**. For us, that's the perfect thousand-mile-long topic of conversation.

If I want my marriage to survive this honeymoon road trip I know I have to stop offering my special helpful **tips for driving in foreign lands**. So now, whenever we are heading into a traffic situation where I think my opinion could be particularly *useful*, I just take a deep breath and close my eyes. I'm learning to be a good wife.

Over the Hill.

Why do old people travel? Why do they bother? I used to feel sorry for old people -- I was 20 and set loose in the world for the first time, once in a while crossing paths with middle-aged couples touring the same château or vineyard as I. I used to pity them -- **didn't they know that travel was wasted on the old?**

Back then, I was the **largest** thing in the landscape. It was my **duty** to go everywhere, see everything in order to verify its reality. For without my witness, the world could not possibly exist in any real way. Old people, they lived in the **past,** a place about which I knew *nothing*, which of course rendered it irrelevant. In travel, life, etc., it was too late for anyone over the age of 40. Wasn't it proof **positive** of their incriminating lack of imagination that they'd waited so long in to get their sorry selves to France? When I, the **Magnificent Vivo**, was already here and *half their age??* I was 20, and the world's most egotistical traveler.

I am acutely aware that I am now the middle-aged traveler that I used to consider so lame, so embarrassing. And I have something to say to my 20-year-old self:

> You cannot possibly know how much time it takes to learn to treasure this world, how many years it takes to properly cherish your place in it.
> As you age, you will find it more and more remarkable, a **miracle**, really, that any of us -- you, me -- are here at all, the result of an undeserved, infinite gift.
> And the older you get, the more you know how much you will **miss.** all this when you are gone.
> In the end, the world was not all that changed by your coming, you were not all that crucial to *it.* But the world, *this* world, which you will one day travel in homage and gratitude, *this* world was **everything** to you.

My Pilgrim Soul.

As much as anyplace can be the Middle of Nowhere in France, the Château de Montaigne is in the middle of nowhere. Technically, it's in the Dordogne region, miles from any place of interest, out on the farthest edge of the bordelaise plain. I'm here to make my pilgrimage to the tower library of the Renaissance philosopher and writer **Michel de Montaigne (1533 - 1592)**.

I stoop to enter through the tiny 13th c. doorway, and I creep up the pitched stone staircase to the gloomy room on the top floor. The bare walls and spare furnishings testify to Montaigne's austere life of the mind. But of course, everyone comes here to see the **ceiling**. My heart pounds as I look up, and see the wooden ceiling beams, *Montaigne's own wooden beams!*, each carved with sayings from the philosopher's favorite classical thinkers -- Pliny, Cicero, Seneca, Plato, Socrates, etc. (described in the home-made English-language guide as the "greeks and latins sentences."

It only takes me ten minutes to absorb the experience -- it's a really, really tiny room. So I turn my attention to the middle-aged woman giving the tour to a five-person group of French tourists. Her speech is the most extraordinary sound I've ever heard. I have a good ear for accents and hers was from the lunar side of normal spoken French. Full of elongated rolling Rs and elaborate throat-clearings with an unusual clipped, patronizing phrasing, her speech reminded me of my meanest French teacher. He said slobby American accents made his ears hurt, and he said that Americans had to build the proper mouth muscles to speak French by reading aloud from Flaubert while biting down on a pencil held between the lips. This lady sounds as if she's taken that pencil and is gargling with it.

I can only stand the sound of her voice for five minutes. And I'm hungry. I leave the tower to find James, who is strolling through the château's vineyards, and we head to Sainte-Foy-la-Grande for lunch.

Beware of **Q**uaintitude.

Quaintitude is found in tourist attractions. It's everywhere, from Papua New Guinea to the Peruvian Andes. It's wherever the word **travel** is preceded by the words **luxury, family, adventure,** or **vacation**. Quaintitude is the easily accessible sentimental consumer experience, a mass-marketed facsimile of a first-hand experience.

France is low on quaintitude. That's because, as explained by Edith Wharton in her book **French Ways and Their Meaning** (1919),

> The French have never taken the trouble to disguise their Frenchness from foreigners.

Sainte-Foy-la-Grande has no quaintitude. It is a very pretty, very old town on the Dordogne River, but it hasn't bothered to put up an amusement park, heritage trail, or a five-star hotel. There isn't a water park in sight, nor an arts festival, craft show, poetry reading, or jazz concert. Especially no jazz. It's totally **real**. We feel ignored, uneventful, and clueless (who was Sainte Foy? Why was she grande?). We like it here very much.

Another Town Without Quaintitude.

St-Macaire is the kind of town to dream of when you dream of packing it all in to go live in France.

First of all, **the size is right**. With a population of 1,500 it's big enough to offer a good variety of interesting neighbors but yet small enough so those neighbors would get to know you and your cats by name.

It's got my favorite kinds of ruins -- **Benedictine** (abbey) and **Plantagenet** (fortifications encircling the town). From 1152 to 1453 the Dukes of Aquitaine were very, very good to St-Macaire and the village grew rich as a port on the Garonne River. But merchants here (major exporters of wine and tobacco to northern Europe) were left, *literally,* high and dry when the river changed course in the 18th century.

So the good news is that since then, **time has passed this village by**. The local wine is the same as ever, (dry white, fruity with peach and blackcurrant flavors). The breeze is the same it's always been, blowing in from the small pine forest nearby and filling the village with the scent of juniper and cinnamon. The going price for a small, 15th-century, two-bedroom house on the main street (see: *right*) is 80,000 € ($100,000).

And then there's *le mascaret,* the last great tidal bore left in France. Great swells of Atlantic sea water from the Gironde roar up the Garonne River, smashing into waves eight feet (2.5 meters) high. The phenomenon used to terrify the locals, back when many of the men were in the long-gone river boat trade, but now the handsome young men of the Aquitaine make a sport of catching the bore at its peak -- when it's just right for **surfing**.

Is that adorable, or what?

The Road Not Taken (theme Song blues).

Cadillac is the title of the best **Johnny Hallyday** song ever. *Cadillac* is also the name of a town on the Garonne River, 17 miles (27 km) south of the city of Bordeaux. And it's the hometown of **Antoine Laumet de La Mothe** (1658 - 1730), founder of **Fort Pontchartrain du Détroit** in the wilds of **New France** (Michigan), the place we Americans now call **The Motor City**.

Lastly, *cadillac* is one of the few French words that sounds much better in English. In English it rolls off the tongue like an onomatopoeia for the way you feel when you're wearing your coolest leather jacket: **cadda-lack**. In French, it sounds like a brand of furniture polish: **caddy-yak**.

Johnny Hallyday, the French Elvis, croons *Cadillac* (the song) with a piercing melodrama, a theatrical blues growl, that breaks my heart. The ache, the desire, the weight of history that he gives *Cadillac* (the song) is all about the longing to be somebody, *a new* somebody in a better place, in the land of dreams:

> *I'm going to scatter myself to America / I'm going to invent laws,*
> *some metal and factories / I'm going to found Détroit.*
> (It sounds much better in un-translated French)

I *love* that song. It makes me cry. That Johnny Hallyday, he can sing. *Cadillac* is the only pop song in the world about how a young French peasant yearned to flee the grime of old Bordeaux and light out for the Americas. You have to admit, that's some deep subject matter for a pop song. And since every road trip needs a good theme song, this one was ours -- *especially* as we drive up and down the Aquitaine, practically in the footsteps of **Antoine Laumet de La Mothe**.

I had every intention of seeing the site of my long-lived **Johnny Hallyday** crush; of, one day, making a side trip to Cadillac. Except that, when that day came, I wasn't in the mood.

James and I had spent much of the day in Saint-Macaire, traipsing through the history and loveliness of the town, imagining us living out the rest of our lives as *Aquitani*. Speculating about such a massive re-invention is extremely tiring.

So when the time came, I did not take the D1113 out of Saint-Macaire, I did not drive ten miles down the road to the hometown of Antoine Laumet de La Mothe. I didn't go to Cadillac. Because all I wanted to do was to park myself with my husband in a cozy café, have a good glass of wine, not deal with any more new information, and then take a nap.

A sudden bout of **road ennui**. It can happen to the best of vagabonds.

Totems

I'll never be able to look at a head of lettuce the same way again.

We come to a screeching halt whenever there is fresh French produce for sale. Every roadside farm stand is a **must see** for James. Every greengrocer is a guru, every barrow boy is a *grand marchand des quatre saisons*. J. loves talking to people who grow, sell, or serve *salade*. But mostly, he loves having a head of it all to himself, to garnish, to dress, to savor.

Every trip has its totem, its **motif**, the thing that stands for the journey itself. Ours is lettuce.

This is James on the beach at **Montalivet-les-Bains** on the Atlantic coast in the Haut-Médoc. It is late morning, and it's hot and J. is wearing his shirt wrapped around his head (whether for comfort or style, I didn't ask). With his Swiss Army knife he's sliced a tomato and a piece of bread and he's piled up his lettuce on a baguette for a pre-lunch snack. Sun, surf, and salad. Seriously, this could be his happiest moment in France.

A Crash Course on French lettuce.

Escarole -- broad leaf endive
Reine des Glaces -- heirloom type with lacy green leaves
Cornet d'Anjou -- curly endive
Kinemontepas -- standard butterhead type
Craquerelle du Midi -- heirloom bibb
Rouge d'Hiver -- red Romaine

JOURNÉE DU *Mercredi*
MARÉE HAUTE
MARÉE BASSE
COEFFICIENT
DIRECTION DU VENT
FORCE
TEMPÉRATURE
EAU 20°
AIR 23°
INFORMATIONS
Chiens et Oursons INTERDIT

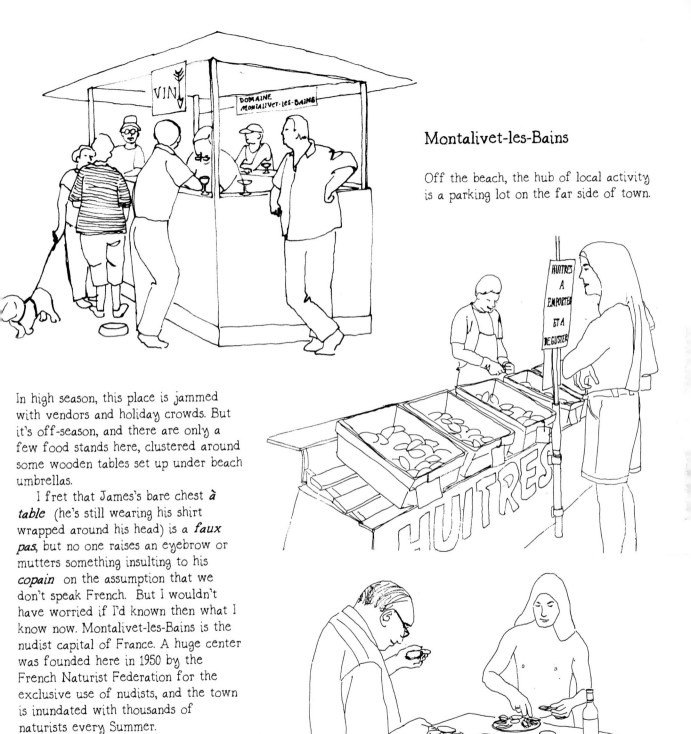

Montalivet-les-Bains

Off the beach, the hub of local activity is a parking lot on the far side of town.

In high season, this place is jammed with vendors and holiday crowds. But it's off-season, and there are only a few food stands here, clustered around some wooden tables set up under beach umbrellas.

I fret that James's bare chest *à table* (he's still wearing his shirt wrapped around his head) is a *faux pas*, but no one raises an eyebrow or mutters something insulting to his *copain* on the assumption that we don't speak French. But I wouldn't have worried if I'd known then what I know now. Montalivet-les-Bains is the nudist capital of France. A huge center was founded here in 1950 by the French Naturist Federation for the exclusive use of nudists, and the town is inundated with thousands of naturists every Summer.

Compared to what these people probably have to look at in high season, James' bare chest is *petites pommes de terre.*

Unifinished Business.

Here's what I see in the rear view mirror: a whole stretch of road from Bordeaux to Cadillac that I should have taken; a view of the Garonne from the left bank that I never saw; a whole town named after *me* (St-Vivien-de-Médoc) that I bypassed; a megalith just south of St-Emilion that I overlooked; the biggest sand dune in Europe that I wish I'd laid eyes on -- and that's only what I missed in the last **week**. But what's a road trip without some regrets? Rejoice in the stones you've left unturned, the road not taken, the **T**s you didn't cross and the **I**s you haven't yet dotted. *That's life.* That's the reason we carry on, take one more chance, never call it quits, *Go West.* That's why I'll always have a reason to hit the road one more time, to come back and do this all again.

A Vacation from the Vacation.

No matter how much in love we are, being each other's constant companion all day, all night, is **unnatural**. And then there's the stress of being in a foreign country: every little thing is a negotiation with language, money, appetites, moods, etc.

One afternoon in **Pauillac** we dither and debate, whether to head farther north on the Médoc peninsula or swing south for a tour of the Graves vineyards. We can't decide which way to go, north or south. After all, there is **nothing** compelling us in either direction, or in *any* direction. And then we look at each other and give up. After all, we're not here to keep a bunch of *appointments.*

"You go get a cup of tea," James tells me, "I'm going to check out the *Maison du Vin.*"

Ah, an hour or two of down time, alone. I sit in a deserted sidewalk café on the *quai* and watch the big container ships rolling slowly down the Gironde to Bordeaux. I write a few postcards, jot some notes in my journal, watch yachts glide into the town's marina.

James joins me just as the sun sinks under the yardarm and orders a glass of wine. We decide to head north.

The waitress brings me the bill and I raise a little hell. 14.70 € for one cup of tea, one glass of red wine! She pretends to study her addition carefully. *"Houp, "* she says, *"I double-charged you!"*

I sigh. I'm back on vacation.

Wayworn

It's our third-to-last night in the Médoc and I have a dream. I dream that suddenly my shoes are too big for my feet. They keep flopping off at every step, making it impossible for me to move. So I fill my socks with mashed potatoes and broccoli. "There," I say; "*Now* those damn shoes'll fit."

Even in my dreams, I know.

Second-to-last night in the Médoc: Late in the day we pull into the driveway of a Bed and Breakfast in Soulac-sur-Mer. The landlady walks out of the house and across the lawn and yells "*Non, non! Park là-bas*, not *ici!*" So James moves the car ten feet over.

The landlady watches with her arms crossed, scowling. I'm thinking that someone who obviously doesn't give a rat's ass about making a good first impression shouldn't be in the hospitality business. I'm also wondering if we should go find other lodgings, but I'm too wayworn to care, really.

And then I see something in the grass, moving towards us. It's a Himalayan cat. I *leap* out of the car, call the kitty to me, and hold her in my arms as if she's my own dear sweet familiar. The cat purrs.

"*C'est bizarre*," the landlady says; "*Normalement*, the cat does not care for people." If ever there was a pot calling a kettle black.

The cat's name is Joy (I heard that right: **Joy**, in English) and she used to belong to the landlady's maiden aunt, who passed away last year. Big surprise: the landlady does not care for cats.

By the look of her house, the landlady cares a great deal for **stuff**, needlepoint pillows and her own oil paintings, cabinets and end tables and shelves crowded with china statues, crystal *anything*, gaudy porcelain eggs, souvenir tea cups. It's as if all this **stuff** is there just to mock anyone who thinks they deserve breathing space in her house. But maybe I'm just tired, and she does have an awfully nice cat, and her husband is a cheerful, welcoming guy who takes good care of Joy. Maybe her **stuff** is just *stuff.*

The next morning there is a big pot of tea and fresh croissants waiting for us in the dining room. Joy sits on my lap the whole time we eat breakfast even though the landlady finds it *pas normal* to have an animal *à table.* I am very happy. It's the best breakfast I've had in all of France.

That's one of the most reliable things about a long road trip. There's always a cat, just when you need one.

This is our last night in the Haut-Médoc, our last stop in Bordeaux wine country. In Vertheuil we find the **Château le Souley**, a vineyard that produces a decent *Cru Bourgeois* wine whose 18th-century *maison* has been turned into a delightful B&B.

It's that golden hour of late afternoon. James pours himself a glass of wine in a go-cup and ambles out to have a look at the town. I wash my hair and set out to look for my husband.

Vertheuil (pop. 1,143) is the kind of place where the so-called *local attractions* are an old church that is 29 kilometers (18 miles) away and a zoo that's 42 km (26 miles) away. In other words, there's nothing actually *in* Vertheuil. This is our kind of place. I find James in front of a closed *boulangerie* and we take a walk twice around the town.

We drive into Pauillac for dinner. My notes say that dinner is *great*, underlined twice; not because of what we ate, but because of the lantern-lit outdoor bistro down near the marina where we had our Farewell to Bordeaux Dinner. We are back in our room by ten o'clock. We wash out some socks and hang them over the window sill to dry, and go to bed. I dream that I live in a cookie factory.

We both wake up at 4AM for some reason. It's so dark, and so still. We open our bedroom shutters and lean out the window and look at the stars. We talk in hushed voices about the next day's travel plans. James is worried that he's lost his beloved Swiss Army knife, the one he's had for 30 years. We'll have to search the car thoroughly before we turn it in tomorrow. No, wait.

It's already **today**.

X
and
Y
The Co-ordinates of
Z en Navigation

X = the limited time you have on the road, in a life

Y = the eternity you have in every hour, every day

Z = Each step you take is a once-in-a-lifetime infinite thing

Bordeaux sketchbook

Only six kinds of grapes are legally permitted to be bottled under the name **BORDEAUX.**

CABERNET SAUVIGNON
the brooding aristocrat,
adds Distinction

MERLOT
the life of the party
adds body & sweetness

the noble **CABERNET FRANC**
for tobacco-raspberry-pepper
finesse

the saucy **PETIT VERDOT**
violet, banana
leather
pencil shavings

MALBEC
the eccentric
dark, aromatic (licorice, toast)
for a deep, plum color

the ethereal **CARMÉNÈRE**
smoky,
spicy, earthy
chocolate and oak

Put them together (but never all six at once) and what you get is

GENIUS.

le Gazé
(Cloaked in gauze)

le Tabac d'Espagne
(Spanish tobacco)

la Petite tortue
(Little tortoise)

le Paon-du-jour
(Peacock of the day)

l'Apollon
(Apollo)

le Petit nacré
(Little pearl)

le Robert-le-Diable
(Robert the Devil)

la Carte géographique
(Map)

l'Aurore
(the Dawn)

le Flambé
(the Blaze)

la Thècle de la ronce
(Saint of the blackberry bramble)

l'Argus
(the Argus)

in Ste-Foy la Grande
an exhibit
of French butterflies!

The Age Old Question: Where Do We Go From Here?

It's Thursday morning in **Bordeaux**. Our plane home to New York leaves from **Paris-Charles de Gaulle Airport** on Monday afternoon. Paris is only 360 miles (582 km) away, a three-hour train ride to **Gare Montparnasse**; there are eight trains today that will get us there. But we've become accustomed to the pace and peace of small towns and neither of us is eager to deal with the bustle of Paris. So let's say we only spend our very last day and night there. That leaves us three days, three nights to hide out in some nice village along the way.

We look at the map. **Tours** is half-way between here and there and J says he'd like to take a day-long bike ride in the Loire Valley. We have a good omen: when we unpacked the rental car we found James's vintage Swiss Army knife that had been missing in action the last couple of days. Things are going well.

There's a train to Tours idling in the Gare St-Jean, ready to leave in 14 minutes. Two and a half hours' travel time, half an hour to orient ourselves, a few minutes to check into one of Tours's charming hotels: we should be settled in our new home base by 3 o'clock this afternoon.

That's the plan for Thursday. We don't know yet what we're doing, exactly, for Friday and Saturday, but we know we have to be in Paris on Sunday. Four days, three nights until it's time for us to *partir*. This is the part of the trip that needs the most strategy, the most careful budgeting of time, now that it's getting more and more finite with each day.

The Countdown to the end of the road has begun.

Postcard from the TGV Bordeaux - St-Pierre-des-Corps

TGV, *Train à Grande Vitesse* (Train of Great Fastness), from Bordeaux to Tours. At 300 km/h (186 mph) top speed the passing landscape is a blur. But train travel is a gorgeous change from car travel -- no steering! No thinking! No deciphering signs, searching for road markers, choosing between equally baffling forks in the road, sussing out back roads that aren't on the map, **NO DECISIONS**. As soon as we got on the train we were carefree again. I really like this kind of travel.

Phase Seven: The End of the Road.

It's a lot like breaking up.

The End of the Road. It's a lot like breaking up.

The Five Signs for Lovers and Travelers That The Thrill Is Gone.

<u>One</u>. You have no interest in relationship-building activities such as romantic dinners, sending love notes.

As James and I head into the Loire Valley, I have very little enthusiasm for this leg of the journey. My apathy has less to do with the fact that this is the fifth or sixth time that I've been through this part of France than with the sad knowledge that there is **nowhere** else to go from here except to the end of the road.

<u>Two</u>. You are baffled by the other's behavior. It's as if you are strangers all of a sudden.

For some strange reason, the train from Bordeaux doesn't go directly into Tours so we have to catch a shuttle into the city. We ask for help from the only ticket agent on duty, and he directs us to an empty platform at the far end of the station. We stand there for 40 minutes before doubt creeps in. We drag ourselves all the way back inside the station to double-check. The ticket agent assures us again that oh yes, *bien sûr,* that is the only *quai* for the shuttle train to Tours. In spite of my horror at asking stupid tourist questions, I bleat "The train, will it come today?" *Aujourd'hui?* the ticket agent repeats, as if taken aback by my audacious curiosity. *Ah non,* he says, in an offended tone of voice: That *train is not running* at all *today!*

<u>Three</u>. Resentment has built up to such a degree that you want to punish the other person with little tit-for-tat retaliations.

The hell with French ticket agents, and the hell with Tours, I fume. I look up at the departure board. There is a train leaving for Azay-le-Rideau in ten minutes.

<u>Four</u>. You are already so detached that you don't even fight for attention and understanding.

It is 5 o'clock when we arrive at Azay, and we haven't eaten since breakfast. We are thirsty, famished, and exhausted. Our first choice of hotel is *complet.* So is our second. At last we get a room in a rickety two-star hotel in the center of town. Numb with fatigue, we are oblivious to Azay's charms. After a quick dinner at a nearby pizzeria, we hole up in our *chambre,* open a bottle of wine, and spend the evening watching TV.

<u>Five</u>. You start to think about life without that person.

This reminds me of when I was desperate to be finished with the Peace Corps at the end of my two-year service in West Africa. Four months before my duty ended, I made a special **countdown** calendar -- a grid of numbers that represented the remaining days of my servitude. I then calculated the total number of **hours** in those remaining **days** and, subtracting the number of hours during which I'd probably be **asleep,** I came up with a running total of the number of **waking hours** I had to endure until I could begin my life without Peace Corps/Africa.

Now that I'm this close to the end of the road in France, it's time to start another **countdown.**

Loire Valley. 57 hours and counting.

COUNTDOWN
Loire Valley Highlights
Top Ten

N̲o̲ 10 My favorite French sight gag: The French don't really care much for nature *au naturel*. They are famously Cartesian -- logical, materialistic -- and that's why they use graph paper to write on (something that shocked me when I bought my first French notebooks 30 years ago). And that's why they landscape their countryside with rows and rows of trees planted in straight lines -- something that I still find hilarious, even after all these years.

N̲o̲ 9 I don't know why I don't do it more often, sit in my French hotel room and watch hours of French TV. At home, I'd never see the like -- a program about German immigrants to Nova Scotia, and a game show that utterly baffles me. (Months later, after its debut on American TV, I realize that the game show is *Deal or No Deal*.) And finally I get the chance to see the classic Cary Grant movie, *Arsenic and Old Lace*, V.O. (in English!).

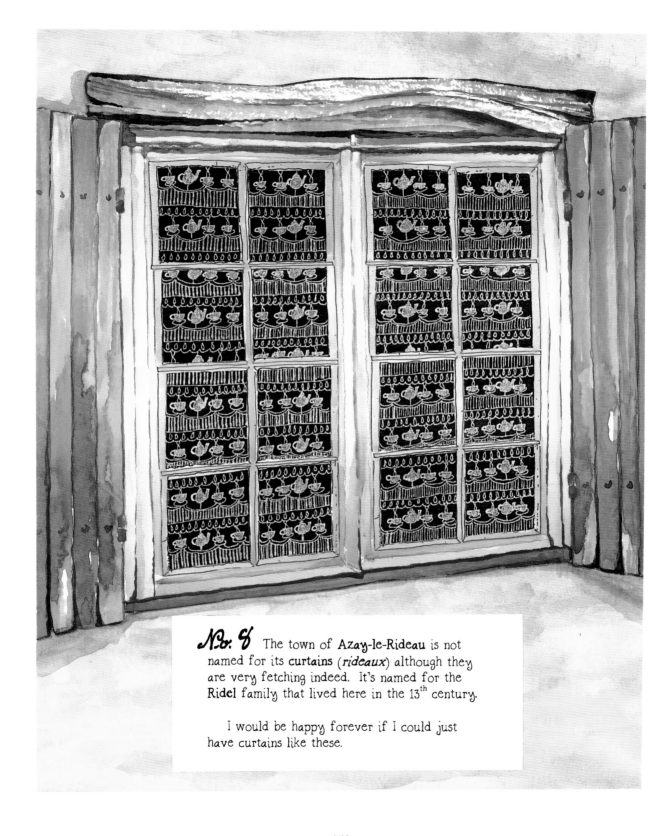

N̶o̶. 8 The town of **Azay-le-Rideau** is not named for its **curtains** (*rideaux*) although they are very fetching indeed. It's named for the **Ridel** family that lived here in the 13th century.

I would be happy forever if I could just have curtains like these.

No. 7 "He just showed up one day," the *patronne* shrugs, "and moved in." I can tell she is a dog person, trying not to admit that she likes the feline company. "*Il s'appelle* Cat," she says, "*The English tourists love him.*" I buy a souvenir refrigerator magnet and take photos of **Cat** posing as the priceless object that he is.

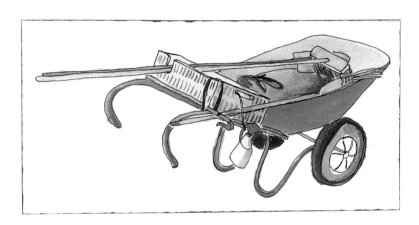

No. 6 This is what it looks like when a man is proud of his work. The street-cleaner of **Azay-le-Rideau** has organized his barrow for maximum efficiency and *finesse.* Two kinds of brooms, a shovel, a litter stick, a bottle of spray-cleaner, a trash bag, a bin for odds and ends of the profession, and everything is in its place. No, he does **not** whistle while he works -- in fact, he scowls at me for peeping into his "office". But then again, what can you expect? He's **French**.

№.5   Customers have to step over the dog to enter the café, a busy meeting place on the main street of **Azay**. But nobody seems to mind. Young and old, they climb over the obstacle on the doorstep, nobody batting an eye or sighing in complaint.

During a lull in business, the *patron* appears in the doorway, wiping his hands on his apron. "I like your dog!" I call out to him. "*Ours*," he corrects me; *Bear.* I laugh. "*Le meilleur,*" he adds: *The best.*

There must be something special about the people of Azay. It's not just the way they have mascots where you least expect them, like this dog, or the cat in the souvenir shop. My friend Barbara tells me that her most vivid memory of Azay, when she came here years ago to meet her elegant French friend's family, was also meeting their pet pig, Eglantine. The pig sat next to her in the parlour when they had tea and nosed into her handbag.

This is my kind of town.

No. 4 The Loire Valley, they say, is a beauty pageant. Each of its castles is a local princess contesting for the title of Queen (the *châteaux*, in every way but grammatically, are feminine).

If you live in the shadow of such *châteaux*, I wonder how you can ever claim to have an **everyday** life.

174

No. 3 There are over 300 *châteaux* in the Loire Valley, some preserved as *patrimoine*, some converted into luxurious hotels, some the private property of reclusive billionaires. This one is **a ruin** and is still the most magnificent of them all: **Chinon.** All because of its chatelaine, the exhausting **Eleanor of Aquitaine.** Heiress/genius/crusader, she became Queen of France at age 15 and ditched it all to run off with Henry II of England -- being French royalty bored her, being the power behind the raucous Plantagenet throne was more to her skill set. How could one woman be responsible for so much history?

I am drawn here because the town glows with the color of *déjà vu.* The architects of Chinon knew that the pale gold building blocks (of a stone called *tuffeau*) would become more beautiful with age, rather like **true love.** And certain legendary queens.

In these limestone cliffs are the caves that the medieval stone masons left behind. Inside, it's always a cool 59° (15 C) with a tangible humidity. It's one of the rarest micro-climates on Earth, found only here and in a secret rainforest high in the Andes. The caves, used for aging vast amounts of local wine, are a mycologist's Eden. Thank the Loire Valley for her mushrooms the next time you order a *sauce chasseur* in Paris.

The **cave dwellers** here are real but rarely seen, which is why some guide books call these remote (but homey) caverns their **hobbit holes.**

Chinon deserves a mindful visit and I'm certainly doing my part, sitting in this café, waiting for James to bicycle in from *qui sait où* and meet me for lunch. He is late, and as Eleanor well knew, there is nothing so quickening as watching for the sight of a beloved husband from on high in Chinon.

№ 2 A Glass of Blessings

Life list -- France

April, Paris: Check.

 Lyricist Yip Harburg admitted to a friend that April was actually a terrible time to be in Paris (too cold, too rainy), and he only wrote about **April** in Paris because **May** didn't scan correctly.

Dancing, Pont d'Avignon: Check.

 On the Pont St-Bénézet, you hold hands and skip to the left.

Starry night, Arles: Check.

 On a clear night, look for Ursa Major, the Whirlpool Galaxy, and the ghost of Vincent.

Toast to LtCom Data, Château Picard vineyard: Check.

 Oh, have some fun. There are worse reasons to drink a $30 bottle of *St-Estèphe Cru Bourgeois* than in honor of the android second officer of the Starship Enterprise.

Glass of Vouvray, banks of the Loire:

In her 1958 novel called **A Glass of Blessings** Barbara Pym wrote about a rare Spring day, one of those special days when the air is especially fine, the light is bright and gentle, the atmosphere full of soothing possibilities. That air, she wrote, is like *"a delicate white wine, perhaps Vouvray, drunk on the banks of the Loire."* I'm a big Barbara Pym fan. So I am not going home until I drink **that** wine in **this** place.

 Check.

№. 1   The Obligatory Proustian Moment.

James never showed up that afternoon in Chinon, but there'd always been that possibility. Any rendezvous on the road is subject to unforeseen conditions *on the road.* So I finished my glass of wine and walked into town to **The Unicorn.** At the only Scottish pub in Chinon, you can count on getting just the right amount of consolation and a good cup of tea. There was cake, too.

When we meet that evening in Azay, James is limping. He crashed his bike near the Château d'Ussé, swerving to avoid an on-coming Peugot in a narrow lane. Still, he'd made it all the way to Villandry and picked up a gift for me: two feathers, found in the famous gardens. We aren't sure, but they could be nightingale.

Our last **Friday night dinner** in France. The menu is pure *pays de la Loire.*

It's not well known but Proust, in fact, did not care much for tea and cake. His appetite was not at all so delicate, and he had a particular love for the hearty specialties of Loire cuisine, wild game and river fish heavily seasoned with local herbs. For James and me, though, leek soup and salad with a cheese course of Loire *chèvres* will do.

There is a radio set on a high corner shelf in the restaurant murmuring bland French pop songs that all sound alike. And then I hear something that I suddenly know every word to. A melody from almost 30 years ago, a song that I'd long forgotten to even **remember.** Background music for travels that took me the farthest from home (in spirit, and miles). Suddenly I remember long lost dance partners, the first time I had caviar, the last time I had Eid al-Adha, snow in Paris, a rainy season in Niger, the sounds of Gamkalé and the Champs Elysées. All those roads, I see now, led to this moment, the way all roads do.

I suddenly feel as if I've been in France forever.

Next Stop: 24 Hours in Chartres.

71 miles (114 kilometers). That's how far it is from Tours to Chartres. In America we call that a hop, skip, and a jump. A piece of cake. A Sunday drive. *Pas de problème.*

"*Non, c'est pas possible,*" the ticket agent at the Tours train station tells me. Even when I show him the official SNCF *horaire* and point out the train that leaves at exactly 12.31 **today**, from **this** train station in **Tours**, and goes all the way to **Chartres**, he says "*Ce train n'existe pas,*" and he refuses to sell me tickets. *C'est tout.* He folds his arms and glares at me.

So I stomp over to the next *guichet* and repeat my request for two tickets for the 12.31 train to Chartres. The new ticket agent promptly sells them to me, 20.40 € each.

In America, being able to **get things done**, especially if it's by bending rules, making exceptions, or calling in a favor, is the way to show power. In France, being able to say *non* (especially to a bureaucratically legitimate request) is the way to show power. *And piss me off.* I march over to the station manager's office and loudly complain about the snotty little ticket agent who thinks it's impossible to go from Tours to Chartres at 12.31 today. I am given an official *SNCF Registre des Réclamations* complaint form to fill out.

I am still fuming when we finally board the 12.31 to Chartres. I've had my **fill** of being on the road, I'm *sick and tired* of being *l'étranger* and not being able to let rip in my **native language**, and I am **fed up** with the French.

At Pezou, a cute teenage couple gets on the train with a cardboard box pet carrier. Gently, the girl sets it on her lap while the boy peers inside, checking that the animal is OK. They both seem very fretful; at last the girl reaches inside and pulls out an angora rabbit. They murmur comforting words and the girl kisses the bunny's head; the boy leans over and rubs noses with it.

A young hipster slouches on board at Châteaudun and I try not to laugh. He's wearing baggy jeans, a baseball cap, and unlaced sneakers, as if he's straight outta Compton. Except he is carrying a dainty tissue paper package tied up in a pink ribbon. Note: it's hard to look **hip-hop** when you're carrying *pâtisseries.*

In spite of myself, I'm enjoying the journey.

A mere two weeks later a letter from *La Chargée de Relation Clientèle SNCF* is delivered to my Long Island home, begging me to believe in the sincerity of the official regrets for my troubles with the ticket agent in the Tours train station. But their apology is too late.

Because by the time our train arrives in Chartres, I'm already back **in love** with France.

I can't help it.

24 Hours in Chartres

Somehow, on all my previous trips to Chartres cathedral, I had completely overlooked its **floor**. But there is a treasure **underfoot**. Set in the stone floor of the nave is one of the world's last in-tact medieval labyrinths. Normally, rows of chairs are arranged in pews on top of the spiral mosaic. But on regularly scheduled days the church workers clear everything away and reveal the 800-year old stonework.

I, however, do not want to see the labyrinth on one of those special days. Because that's when the cathedral is mobbed, and I do *not* want to get stuck behind those show-off penitents who "do" the Chartres labyrinth on their **knees**. No, I want the labyrinth all to myself. So I've come here on one of its **off** days.

James helps me push some chairs out of the way and I kneel to touch the stones. Think of all the symbolic journeys to Jerusalem that have been made in these worn pathways, think of all the prayers that have smoothed these Berchères paving stones. Think deep thoughts until a church warden comes to yell at you to put the chairs back.

The Chartres labyrinth is 41 feet (12.455 meters) wide. The 11-circuit path is 860 feet long (1/6th of a mile, 262 meters); it takes an hour to creep the distance on the patellas. And the path is only 13 inches (33 cm) wide. No passing lane.

Chartres comes as a shock to me. The last time I was here, in 1992, the town was still recognizable as the same dusty, run-down burg that I'd first visited in 1975. It was still the same Chartres that had taught me, 30 years ago, that not every shop in France was *entrée libre*. I'd been browsing (five minutes? ten?) at an *alimentation* on the Rue de la Couronne when the shop owner decided I'd been there a little too long and he **exploded**, hurling French words at me in a shock wave of rage. Then he grabbed a ladle from one of his vats of *crème fraiche* and waved it in my face as I backed out of his doorway. In good old Ye Olde Chartres, shopping was not part of the democratic process. You were **not** guaranteed an *entrée libre* -- the freedom to enter a shop and not buy anything.

But I liked old-time Chartres exactly *because* it was *so* French; cranky, time-worn, touchy about the social hierarchy. I never held its Frenchness against it.

But now, Chartres is booming. The old dirt *boules* grounds near the train station have been enlarged, paved, landscaped, and dignified as **plazas**. Roads have been widened, shop fronts have been painted, new hotels have been built. The streets around the cathedral have been closed to automobiles, paved over and re-purposed as a **pedestrian shopping mall**. And today those streets are crowded with Saturday afternoon shoppers, young mothers jostling their baby strollers, tourists holding up foot traffic, teenagers traveling in noisy packs of four and five -- *teenagers!* Loud, rude, flirty, under-dressed **teenagers**, where once the only sign of life on these dank back streets would have been the shadow of a stray cat, the echo of retreating footsteps. Jeeze. Now, in Chartres, I might as well be back home on Long Island.

James steps into a *fromagerie*. He is, as usual, inspired by artisanal cheese. I am, as usual, overwhelmed by the smell, and also by the way my archaic memories of Chartres are being assimilated by this new, shiny, Chartres-Borg. James putters up and down the aisles looking for a nice *chèvre*, and I wait for him near the *caisse*. Of course we have *l'entrée libre*. I stare at the cheese on display, idly noting the price tags, so many *euros* for so many *kg*. A melancholy is gathering in me, some vague regret which I can't pinpoint until I meet the doleful eyes of the cheesemonger.

"This is my first visit to France since the switch to the Euro," I say to him, *"C'est triste, d'être en France sans le franc."*

I said I was **sad** to be in France **without** the franc because if I'd said what I'd really meant to say, that I miss the franc, I'd have to use the loathsome French verb *manquer* in a sentence with myself as the direct object -- the French have a very weird way of saying they miss things or people -- so I always avoid it whenever I can. But to tell you the truth I hadn't really been bothered by the demise of the French franc until now. Now, though, it **does** make me sad.

And I'm embarrassed to have blurted out this little confession to a French shopkeeper (such intimate small talk between retailer and client is not an established ritual in France, as it is in America). So the cheesemonger's sympathetic response surprises me. *"Chez nous, c'est triste aussi,"* he says; and he, too, looks sad: *"Everything changes."*

I see in his eyes the sadness of all of us who feel left behind by our memories. Me, by the 20-year-old self that I last saw in Chartres in 1975, he by the 90% of French people who -- *quelle horreur!* -- are eating **supermarket** cheese these days.

But then I see my husband, and he's got a big smile on his face (there is a lot of *fromage de chèvre fermier* to choose from in Chartres), and I am roused from my reverie. Everything changes, but sometimes for the better. For instance, I have this nifty new traveling companion, which is much better than having globs of *crème fraiche* splattered in your face.

Dear Reader:

France is a fun country to illustrate. And I've taken great delight in picturing it all for you, showing you the marvelous things I've seen, the landscapes and *animaux* and *objets*, in shop windows, on the menu, down the road, behind the scenes.

But this (see above) is the picture I **most** enjoyed painting. I was **so** careful to get the color of the sky just right (it was the first **sunset** that felt like Fall in France; mild but with a new chill in the air). I fussed to get the correct number of *étages* in the cathedral towers, the proper slants to the Chartres rooftops. I paid close attention to the hinges of our hotel room window (which is necessary when you have **real** French windows, which open into the room). I tried very hard to paint James as handsome as he is in real life, and I had to make sure I got him holding his beloved Swiss Army knife.

I obsessed about rendering our banquet in detail: James's final **Road Trip Salad**, my take-out dish of *carottes râpées*, the slice of *pâté en terrine*, the baguette, oh! The pink ribbon on the tissue-paper puff that's holding my dessert *pithiviers!* Can you see how lovingly I've painted it all?

It is Saturday night in Chartres, a fine September evening in 2005, our next-to-last night on the road. These French foods are the ones I'll most miss, this hotel room view is the one I'll never forget, this man is why I love my life.

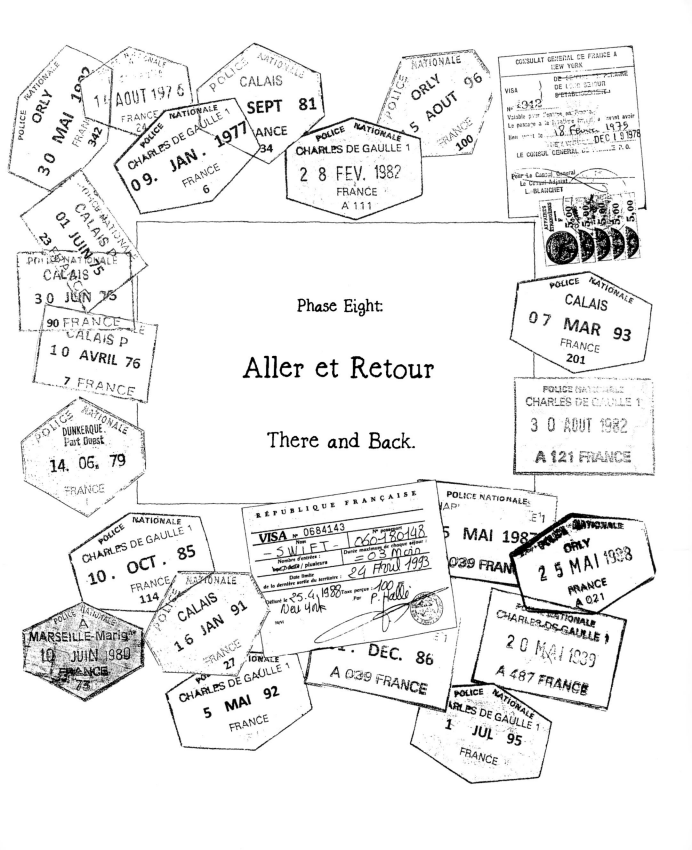

Phase Eight:

Aller et Retour

There and Back.

Aller et Retour.
(There and Back.)

We can't stop falling in love.
The statistics prove it:

- 75% of people in the United States will marry at least once.
- 75% of divorced people will re-visit marriage: 54% of them will re-marry within the first five years of their divorce.
- 12% of men and 13% of women will marry twice in their lifetime.
- 3% of men and women will marry three times or more.

from the National Center
for Health Statistics, 2002

We can't stop traveling.
The statistics prove it:

- This year (2005), travelers like James and I will venture to foreign places 842 million times.
- That number will increase by 100 million travelers in the next five years.
- There are 193 countries in the world, but one out of every twelve travelers roaming the globe will be heading to France (everybody's favorite foreign country).
- According to the French Government Tourist Office (*Atout France*), two thirds of those who travel to France are repeat visitors.

from the United Nation's
World Tourism Organization report for 2005

For lovers and travelers, one thing is for sure:
We always come back.

Paris,
The Final 24 Hours.
Back where we started.

It is startling, at first, after several weeks in the country, to be back in the capital. The crowds, the noise, the scale of life here is too busy, too loud, and too grand.

But after checking into our hotel and taking a brisk walk through the 7th *arrondissement* we feel more in sync with the city. And a long walk on the Quai d'Orsay helps us ward off the moodiness that comes on when you are making your farewells to Paris.

It's midafternoon, Sunday, a bit of Summer still left in the air. Tomorrow we catch an afternoon flight back to New York City.

And tomorrow, back here in Paris, come the Green Hour, our seats at café Les Deux Palais will be empty.

Tomorrow, when the late afternoon sun glows silver on the Seine, the shine will warm others' souls.

Tomorrow, a blue silken evening will settle over a Paris without us.

Without us.

So today is all about memorizing these last few hours.

Today is all about taking our long last good-byes.

Starting with a farewell croissant.

Why do we travel?

There are probably as many reasons as there are travelers. But based on the travelers I have known, and on my own reading of some of the most popular current guide books and travel magazines, these seem to be the

Top Five Reasons to Travel:

1. To shop. *
2. To see in person the things we have only seen on TV. *
3. To have our pictures taken in front of famous stuff. *
4. To escape our troubles. **
5. To interact with people we have long had a great curiosity about. ***
6. For the croissants. ****

* 1, 2, and 3: In a word, TOURIST.
** 4. True for people who journey to either tropical beaches or war zones.
*** 5. This is what separates the shoppers from the **travelers**.
**** 6. And when we fail to achieve 100% culturally authentic interactive travel, there's always **croissants**.

James discovers the Smart Car.

"I want to put it in my pocket
and take it home with me!"

Sentimental Journey

Why **do** we travel? I'm not sure that I travel for profound reasons, or even if profound reasons are necessary. Why do we fall in love? (I have my reasons, you have yours.) All I know for sure (about love and travel) is that the joys last a lifetime, and the woes are always worth it.

I am certainly ready to leave France. This journey has run its course, hit all the unforgettable highs and lows, so many present moments turned into memories, and (maybe) some bits of wisdom. But you know how it goes. We haven't even left French territory and already we are talking about the **next** trip.

Travel, love, life. It's all the same mapping expedition. J. and I, leaving France, take with us a new mental map of ourselves -- dominions newly discovered, boundaries re-drawn, the named territories wider and deeper than those we knew before. Thank you, France, *Merci*, and Good-bye.

    Oh, wait.

    There's still that one last *au revoir.*

Souvenirs from Le Road Trip

Sand	Gravier	Clay	Garonne gravel	Tuffeau
from Omaha Beach	from Saint-Malo	from St-Emilion	from the Haut-Medoc	from Chinon

Acknowledgments

Emily Marlin wrote the book *Taking a Chance on Love* that helped me articulate the theory on love and travel that made this book possible. The fact that she's also my **aunt** makes me one ridiculously lucky niece!

Joan Fisher is a *real* world traveler, and an inspired every-day adventurer. She's the only person I know who can start out on a neighborhood stroll in Manhattan and end up in Berlin. When she showed me her fabulous inventions, the pocket-sized travel scrapbooks that she's made of her various round-the-world trips, I knew I *had* to have them in my book (on page 7).

Thank you also to:

Carol Danforth, my advisor on all things elegant and Alabama.
Deborah S. Farrell, winged inspiration in human form.
Barbara Finwall /Banar Designs, whose delicious taste and humor are reflected in her own
        beautiful books.
Gitana Garofolo, such a *grande dame* that I think she must be a re-incarnated Plantagenet.
Maryann Gastaldo, a kindred traveler in the *beaux arts*.
Cheryl Gebhart, an artist to the core.
Rachel Kopel, the West Coast Woman of Spirit.
Janet Lea, traveler, writer, ally: the Texas warrior princess with a Parisian soul.
Candice Ransom, author and Southern Belle who knows how to get book-writing *done.*

Don't underestimate the benefits to your writer's morale of having friendly, professional, and hilarious guys running the UPS store (with its killer photocopier); Thank you, **Frank Scarangella** and **Frank Scarangella Jr.**

Joe Molloy, thank you for that fateful conversation about your father, James A. Malloy, that brought me to Omaha Beach, the 29ers, and changed my life.

To the 29th Division, veterans of the D-Day invasion on Omaha Beach on June 6-7, 1944 whose historic 115th, 116th, and 175th Infantries fought from Normandy to the Rhineland in WWII: I thank you for your service and your friendship. For their help in my research on the life and death of 29er James A. Malloy, C Co., 175th Inf., I must thank in particular:
Joseph Balkoski, 29th Division Historian.
Harold Beukelaer, C Co., 175th Infantry (James Malloy's best friend).
Ivan Dooley, CW4 (Ret), of the Maryland Military Historical Society.
William Doyle, T/Sgt, Company leader, C Co., 175th Inf., and Chevalier de l'Ordre National de la Légion d'Honneur.
Donald McKee, Med. 2nd Bn, 175th Inf., Past President of the 29th Division Association and editor of the The Twenty-Niner, published by the 29th Division Association:
To perpetuate the friendships we cherish;
to keep alive the spirit that never knew defeat;
to glorify our dead, and to further keep before our country
the record of the 29th Division in the World Wars.

29: Let's Go!

Chère Madame Benedicte Canielle, seeker, dreamer, thinker (a real-life archetypical Artist-Scientist) saved me from my delusions of grandeur (I had the nerve to think I was fluent in French). Thank you for your gracious oversight of all things Français in this book.

At Bloomsbury Kathy Belden is the *Editor Exemplaire* who did everything she could to make this book (and its author) classy. Keely Latcham's *assistance* was *extraordinaire*.

Betsy Lerner wrote the book that made me an author: *The Forest for the Trees* gave me all I needed to know about the art and business of writing so that I could become a published writer. Also, she's the only agent I ever dreamed of working with... having her for an agent is like winning the Oscar/Nobel/MacArthur Genius Award -- she's *that* good. Thank you.

Final Travel Tip: Before you leave home, put a bottle of champagne in the fridge. So when you drag yourself back from the glories and adventures of Le Road Trip, you'll have something to make *la rentrée* and the unpacking seem fun. Or, at least, not so depressing.

Irving Stone (1917 - 1978)
Dorothy Stone (1919 - 2005)
In Paris, France, 1957

My husband's parents, jet-setters from Long Island, didn't **travel**.
They **went abroad**.
Dressed to kill.
Thank you for going while the getting was good,
and for bringing back the photos.

On the flight home, James and I discussed our next Road Trip.
Ach, crivens! We're packing for **Scotland!**